FROM POLE TO POLE
WITH A FEW STOPS BETWEEN

A Collection of Stories
and Poems

HARRY HANLAN

Scott

I hope you enjoy my book

Thanks

Harry Hanlan

 FriesenPress

Suite 300 - 990 Fort St
Victoria, BC, V8V 3K2
Canada

www.friesenpress.com

#34 Transportation Safety Board of Canada
#35 Boeing of Canada,de Havilland Division
Page 94 Antarctic Journal of 1994

ISBN
978-1-5255-3428-7 (Hardcover)
978-1-5255-3429-4 (Paperback)
978-1-5255-3430-0 (eBook)

1. Biography & Autobiography, Personal Memoirs

Distributed to the trade by The Ingram Book Company

For Margo

Table of Contents

About the Author

Harry started flying in 1967 and worked along the north coast of British Columbia for various logging companies until 1972. During that period, he also owned his own airplane and flew skydivers out of Terrace, British Columbia. In 1972, Harry moved to Alberta and went to the Arctic with Northward Airlines, flying Single and Twin Otters out of Inuvik, Norman Wells, and the high Arctic. In 1974, he hired on with Gulf Oil, flying a Twin Otter out of Inuvik doing rig support in the Mackenzie Delta. In July of 1977, he started with Kenn Borek Air in Resolute Bay, which began a twenty-six-year career, working around the world doing mostly off-strip work on tundra tires, floats, and skis. The first of many trips to the North Pole was in 1978 in support of Naomi Uemura, the Japanese adventurer. In 1981, Harry took a Twin Otter to South America and flew there under contract for a Canadian oil company. The first of many trips to Antarctica was in 1984, flying a Twin Otter for the National Science Foundation of the USA. This assignment involved ferrying the aircraft from Calgary to the Antarctic, via the west coast of South America to Punta Arenas, Chile, and across the Drake Passage to Antarctica where the aircraft supported scientists all over the continent during the austral summers. He spent one season flying a DC-4 out of Punta Arenas to Antarctica for a tourist operation. During these years, he also flew in Vanuatu doing scheduled runs for a local airline and in Kyrgyzstan, flying for a Canadian mining company. Harry ferried a Twin Otter from Calgary to Rangoon, Burma, in 1990, which was the first of many contracts in that country. After a ferry trip to the Maldives in 1997, he stayed and flew Twin Otters on floats for a tourist operation. Harry retired from commercial flying in 2003 after a serious collision on a highway in Southern Alberta.

His log book records show the following:

20,000 plus hours on Twin Otters

3,000 plus hours on Single Otters

500 hours on a DC-4

300 hours on a Beech 99

5,000 hours on Cessna 172,180,185, 206, Maule, and Norseman

Glossary

The following terms and wording, which are used in these stories, might be unfamiliar. Some definitions might help.

Horizontal stabilizer - Is like a small wing at the rear of the aircraft

Elevator - A control surface that is attached to the horizontal stabilizer and controls nose up or down motion

Vertical stabilizer - The section of the tail that the rudder is attached to

Rudder – A surface that controls left and right movement

Empennage - The rear part of an aircraft that is comprised of the four previously listed items

Aileron – A control surface that is attached to the outer section of a wing to control bank

Clag - A slang term that pertains to low cloud, bad weather, fog, or any other condition that causes visual difficulty for a pilot

C-130 - A 4-engine transport aircraft called a Hercules. Operated on skis for the National Science Foundation by the U.S. Navy (at the time this was written)

I.F.R. - Instrument Flight Rules. The ability to fly an aircraft with no visual reference to the ground

Bleed air valves - Control a supply of heated, pressured air to the cabin. We used the pressured air to operate the in-flight refueling system

N.S.F. - National Science Foundation

B.A.S. - British Antarctic Survey

Traverse - A route or trail across a glacier or mountain slope

Boondoggle - A frivolous non-productive venture

I.L.S. - Instrument landing system that allows an aircraft to be positioned in a landing position without reference to the ground

Outer marker - A positioning point on an instrument approach

Parkall - An insulated canvas-covered framework that is used for temporary camps in the Arctic. The same framework is called a Jamesway in Antarctica

M.O.T. - Ministry of Transport

R.C.M.P. - Royal Canadian Mounted Police

I have tried to break this book into time periods and different locations. There will be some overlap as there were many return contracts over the years.

First Incident

I guess the first incident of any consequence in my flying life was in 1967— a two-year interruption of a fishing trip that we had planned to northern Saskatchewan.

Ed, my flying instructor and good friend, and I had planned the trip for a few weeks, and on the day of departure out of Calgary, we agreed to drop one of Ed's students at his family farm in Melfort on our way to La Ronge.

The day was fine and clear as we dropped down to check out the road in front of the farmyard. It looked OK for a landing, and we circled back to land. Gear down, full flap, the Comanche at seventy knots and looking good when the power line hit the windscreen.

Things happened fast from that point; the line slipped over the roof and started sawing into the tail as the line tore loose from the pole in the farmyard. The last thirty feet wrapped around the top of the stabilizer and sliced down the length of the cabin with a crack like a rifle shot, opening the skin like a knife. The last of the wire cut off the top of the stabilizer and jammed the rudder solid as the plane crowded the fence to the left of the road and slowly climbed to a safe height. We decided, after returning to survey the amount of aluminum scattered along the road, that with no rudder and unsure of the extent of the damage, we had better land on the now clear road.

The lady from the farmhouse showed us where we could park the aircraft then asked us in for coffee. I looked at her electric stove and suggested that a cold drink would be a better bet.

The damage to the aircraft was sufficient enough to park it for some months while a rudder and stabilizer were located and flown in from Panama. The student decided to become a farmer and never returned to the flying club. If the line had gone under the prop spinner instead of above it?! Yeah well!

Figure1. Damage to the aircraft from hitting a power line

Figure 2. Damage to the aircraft from hitting a power line

Months later when the rudder and stabilizer arrived in Calgary, we loaded the parts in a brand, new Chrysler that belonged to our friend Ray and headed for Saskatchewan to rescue the aircraft.

In Drumheller, while Ed and I hit the liquor store, Ray circled the block. Then, we were on our way.

Halfway up the hill, a red light behind us caused some concern, and the local R.C.M.P. officer pulled us over for turning on a red light, which is allowed in Calgary, but not in Drumheller. "Any booze in the car?" he asked. Well, we knew damn well he knew the answer to that, so we owned up to what we had purchased as we were on our way to a wedding party. "We will be checking you further down the line," he said, "so keep it sealed."

Well that scared us bad enough to not have a beer 'till the top of the hill. By the time we hit Rosetown, Saskatchewan, we were in pretty good shape with Ed asleep in the back seat.

Pulling into a drive-through restaurant for some burgers, we were cut off by a '56 Ford with four locals in it. I mouthed a few obscenities at them and told them to get out of the way or else. This was all done with the window up, but when they asked what I had said, Ray rolled down the window and repeated it word for word. We got our burgers and hit the highway with these jerks on our tail. After a few miles at about one hundred miles an hour, I told Ray that we had better stop and get our licking or someone was going to die. As we coasted to a stop, a second car with two more locals pulled in behind us. "Oh man, we are in trouble," I said as this group approached. "Better get Ed up."

"Are you sure we want to do that?" questioned Ray. "Last time he took that guy's eye out with a beer bottle. He goes out of control when he's been drinking."

Ed crawled out of the back door with this fringed buckskin jacket with a stuck zipper, trying to get it off over his head and shouting, "If we have to fight, let's get at it."

The first car with the four guys screeched a U-turn on the highway and was gone. The two guys in the second car explained that they only stopped to see if there was a problem, and they are gone. Ray and I were leaning on the hood of his new Chrysler, all alone, looking at the stars, and counting our lucky ones. "Where's Ed?" Ray asked, and we started looking around. Ed crawled out of the ditch covered with mud and still wrapped in this damn jacket. Some help he would have been! Ray's new car the next morning was a mess, two inches of rum and Coke splashing around in the console box, mud from Ed all over the back seat and rear deck, but no blood.

We repaired the aircraft, Ed flew it home, and Ray and I drove. We stopped for fuel just east of Rosetown, and the lady at the gas station said, "Hey boys, I hear you got your airplane fixed."

"Yes," we said, "and we are on our way home."

"Don't stop in Rosetown," she cautioned. Man, small world, that Saskatchewan.

Two years later, with the aircraft repaired and repainted, Ed and I did do the fishing trip.

Terrace, British Columbia—Highway Landing

My first flying job was in Terrace, British Columbia in 1969, flying a Cessna 180 on floats for a west coast logging company. We later upgraded to a Cessna 185.

The mountain passes into Terrace were all thick with smoke as I tried to get into the Kitimat Valley from the east. Finally, I had to double back to the Skeena River and come in from the north. I was flying a Cessna 180 on floats, from Prince George and, with the time lost trying to get through the passes to the south, I was getting more than a little low on fuel. With the low visibility, I descended to avoid any conflict with the 737 that was inbound on the approach, and, as I levelled out over the ridge that drops into the Seaplane Base, the engine quit. I had no altitude to play with, a set of high tension power lines to get over, and the Terrace-Kitimat Highway below.

Stretching the glide to the limit, I barely cleared the power lines as I flashed my landing lights at two oncoming vehicles. The second car pulled off into a turnout, and as I passed over the first car, the folks flashed their lights and waved. I'm sure the floats cleared their trailer by only inches as I landed behind them and scraped to a grinding halt on the pavement. The car never stopped, and I found out later that my wife's mom and dad told her that I had buzzed them on my way into the lake. They were on their way home from a visit with us and were totally unaware that I had landed behind them on the road. The other car approached slowly, and the woman driver's first question was, "Did you land here on purpose or what?" Not sure what my answer was.

Figure 3. Cessna 180, CF-JCQ sitting on the Terrace - Kitimat highway after an emergency landing

Figure 4. Cessna 180, CF-JCQ sitting on the Terrace - Kitimat highway after an emergency landing

With the help of the local carrier, I had the aircraft on a trailer and towed to the airport. When I checked the keels of the floats, I found that, other than a bit of wear, nothing was damaged. I flew it off a dolly and back to the lake the next morning. Nothing was ever heard from the Ministry of Transport, and if it wasn't for the *Highway Harry* nickname that still comes back to haunt me, the whole incident would be forgotten. The 737 pilot had heard my mayday and circled until I called and told him I was down safely.

Two weeks later while I was chatting up a stew on my way to Vancouver, she confided that, "The Terrace flight is usually quite boring, but a few weeks ago some guy in a little airplane..." I denied any knowledge of the incident and went back to my book.

Winter Float Operations—Terrace, British Columbia

We were still parked on the lake when winter set in with a vengeance. The weather was too bad to take off and fly to the airport, which was a few hundred feet higher than the lake the lake. The lake froze over and about fifteen inches of snow accumulated before we got a break in the weather to move. After chopping free of the ice, I took off on the snow and landed beside the runway where we put the plane on a trailer, hangared it for the winter, then put it on a dolly for takeoff when the lake opened in the spring. There were no brakes on the dolly at that time, and it managed to wipe out three runway lights before stopping.

Figure 4a. CF-WEE early winter on Lakelse Lake, Terrace, British Columbia. 1969

Figure 5. CF-WEE dolly takeoff. Spring, 1970

Leaving British Columbia for the Northwest Territories

Flying the west coast of British Columbia on floats was a lot of fun, but the logging industry seemed to be plagued by strikes of some group or another, and I was often off work while they were settled. I sold my Cessna 172 that I had been using for the local skydivers and moved back to Alberta in 1972 to do some crop-dusting with a friend of mine. While there, I approached two companies that flew in the Northwest Territories. Within hours, I had offers from both of them. My float experience was in great demand, and the next day I was headed for the Arctic. I loved it. I flew a Single Otter in Inuvik for a few months, then moved to Norman Wells where I spent three years flying Single Otters and Twin Otters. Long trips in slow airplanes were the cause of the poems scattered throughout this book. I flew for Northward Airlines from June 1972 to mid-September 1974, working out of Inuvik, Norman Wells, and on a three-month contract in the high Arctic in the spring of 1973.

Inuvik

I knew it was north, but not much else. It was June of 1972, and I was scheduled to leave Edmonton on the following day to start work for Northward Airlines, flying a Cessna 206 out of Yellowknife. The phone call at midnight was to ask if I would consider going to Inuvik to fly a Single Otter instead, because the 206 was still in maintenance. "Would I mind?" In Terrace, British Columbia, where I had been flying, the chief pilot flew the Single Otter, and the chance of ever getting left seat in it was very remote, yet here it was. "Would I mind?"

The next morning, I boarded a Pacific Western Airlines flight to Yellowknife where I met up with Bert Fraser who I would be flying with for the next two weeks. Yellowknife to Norman Wells, pick up a load of groceries for Fort Good Hope, then on to Inuvik. It was hard to get used to the twenty-four-hour sun. At 2:00 a.m. when we arrived, the sun was shining brightly, and the baseball diamond was full of kids. This was before television of course. Checking into the McKenzie Hotel some twenty hours and over one thousand miles from home, we gratefully passed out for the *night*. The base manager met us in the lobby the next morning at 8:00 with a handshake and a can of OFF— very funny 'till we stepped outside. OFF was to be a constant companion and number one item on our preflight checklist 'till late fall. The next ten days became a fascinating blur of trips: passenger and grocery runs to Aklavik, Fort McPherson, Arctic Red River, and Tuktoyaktuk; fuel and camp supplies to lakes and rivers from the barrens to the Yukon.

One morning while our airplane was down for maintenance, I met the pilot of the other company Otter who was working off Shell Lake. "Eldon, is that you under that beard?" Eldon, an old friend from Calgary, quickly arranged for me to accompany him on an extended fuel haul trip to Old Crow in north central Yukon.

After three to four 16-hour days, we began to *leg about*—one of us flying and the other sleeping in the back, in a sleeping bag that was laid out on a half-sheet of plywood and placed on top of the drums. This arrangement enabled us to go nonstop with meals—well, sandwiches and cookies that were brought to the dock by the camp cooks during loading or unloading periods and enjoyed leisurely in flight. Three more trips into a new location and we would be returning to Inuvik.

Circling the small, algae-covered lake, it was impossible to see into the green, scummy water, but the camp had a small pier running out into the lake. Eldon crawled sleepily into the right seat and told me that he had worked for this crew the year before, and the men seemed to know what they were doing. With that, I turned to line up with the dock, dropped full flaps, and touched down fifty feet from the shore. As the plane came down off the step, we lurched once, then came to an abrupt halt about the center of this circular pond. "Great!" was one of the few printable words that I heard as I shut down the engine. We both stepped out on the floats. "What are you guys trying to do to me?" Eldon roared, as we watched two men in waders plow their way toward us from the dock. They seldom went over their knees in this bog-bottomed, mosquito-infested swamp.

"I had no idea you needed that much water," the new-to-the-north party manager groaned, as I explained the required thirty inches. "How are we going to get the rest of our fuel and groceries in?"

"That's the least of our worries," Eldon bellowed. "How the hell am I going to get this airplane out of here?"

While tempers cooled, I untied the four barrels of Helo fuel and dumped them into the water while the others tramped out in front of the airplane, hoping to find some deeper water. No luck. "Have you run into any rocks at all?" Eldon asked.

"No, just this damn mucky bottom all over," was the reply.

"If we can get moving, we might just be able to do it," Eldon mused, mostly to himself. Moving two of the barrels off to one side and standing them up provided a bit of an area to set the case of eggs and meat on. We agreed that if we got airborne we would find a suitable place on the Porcupine River about eight miles away to drop the remaining supplies; a big *if* it looked like to me.

"Your leg, Eldon," I said as I strapped myself into the right seat.

"Thanks," he growled and hit the starter. Six blades, mags on, and the Pratt and Whitney 1340 rumbled into life. Takeoff check completed, there would be no stopping if we got moving. Powering to takeoff power, we sat for ten to fifteen seconds, pushing and pulling on the control, trying to break free. Power back, idle for a few minutes, then shut down, and back on the float. "If we can break it free, I think it will go." Eldon grunted as the four of us pushed our feet deeper into the mud, trying with no success to move the aircraft back a few inches. While I pumped the floats for the second time, Eldon tied a fifty-foot piece of rope to the back bollard. "If you fellows can pull sideways on the rope while I try to rock it with full power on maybe…" With the engine roaring, the control column rocking the aircraft back and forth, and the men heaving on the rope, the Otter slowly started to move in an ungainly motion—forward three to four feet, lurch, slow down, lurch again. Turning slowly to parallel the shore, we slowly ground our way in a gentle curve, picking up speed then losing some as we dragged across the shallows. Ever so slowly, we picked up speed, and as we completed a circle of the lake, we came up on the step and then into the air.

The tension and sweat drained off us as the stagnant water dripped from our boots, pooling in the rudder wells. "I think we got the best of that deal," I laughed. Eldon banked to see what I was finding so amusing and broke into a wide grin. In the middle of the lake were two small figures, each with a cardboard box on one shoulder, fighting their way through the soft-bottomed muck. "Hope they enjoy that food. I bet each of those boxes will weigh 150 pounds by the time they get them to shore."

Back in Inuvik that evening for the first time in ten days, we headed to the bar to meet with the rest of the crews. Smiles of welcome on every face should have warned us that something was up. That and the fact that each of the eighteen people at our table ordered a double slipped by us until the waitress presented Eldon and me with the bill of just over a hundred dollars. "Flying home with your rear tie-down rope trailing," roared the base manager.

"But... but... but," I stammered, as Eldon dug an elbow in my ribs.

"Shut up, we'll split the bill, and hope they never hear the rest of the story."

I.F.R.

I think about the time I spent

With Single Otter, yet content

To fly above the trees, but just.

For stay below the clouds, you must.

I'd fight my way through driving rain

To do the trip, then back again.

Or watch the rime ice slowly grow,

And strain my eyes through blowing snow,

To try and keep the ground in sight,

While looking for the runway lights.

Now looking down from high above,

Twin I.F.R. I really love.

Twin Otter on Floats

A Twin Otter on floats is the greatest float plane ever built. With total control on the water, docking is simple, and with a good crewman even the worst conditions can be handled. Having said that, let me relate an instance that took place on Great Bear Lake in the fall of '73. My co-pilot crewman, who we will alias as Dougie, had been with me for a couple weeks and seemed to be working out quite well. Or, so I thought. . . .

Figure 6. A Twin Otter on floats, a wonderful machine.

The oil company had laid a pipe rack out into the lake to act as a dock on the north shore. No protection of any type for the floats, a wind quartering across the dock, and a large wave pattern running in to shore, would make the docking a challenge. Added to that was a sandbar —shallow enough to drag on and about thirty feet in front of the pipe rack. What we had to do was drive in across the sandbar, turn the aircraft, and back into the downwind side of the pier. Oh, did I mention that the shoreline was all big boulders? Well,let's get into the story.

We landed in some large waves, turned to taxi downwind, and bounced across the sandbar. We got turned around and backed the rear of the float close enough to tie off to the dock. The wind direction was such that I could only hold that position for a few moments. Dougie was learning the hard way that you cannot hold a Twin Otter with just one wrap around the pipe.

I left him on the dock as I taxied out over the sandbar to deep water and crawled out onto the float to retrieve the tie-up rope. I bounced back over the sandbar, nosed into the dock, threw him the rope, made a tie-up sign with my hands, then proceeded to turn around and again attempted to back into the dock. This time, Dougie managed to get two wraps around the pipe. With the large surface of the tailplane and a twenty- to thirty-knot wind, the result was exactly the same as the first time. This time when I got out to the deep water, I shut down the engines and, as I retrieved the rope, I yelled at Dougie, "TIE IT OFF, YOU CANNOT HOLD IT." I drove in over the sandbar, again threw the rope to the dock and maneuvered the rear of the float toward the dock. It's a tough stretch to look back and work the power levers, and my curses were drowned by the scream of the turbines as I saw that Dougie had tied the rope to the dock and was now trying to catch the float bollard with an eighteen-inch piece of rope. Well, of course, that didn't work, and as I was turning around for try number four, a roughneck came down to help. Dougie jumped to the float and hooked to the bollard while the roughneck tied off to the dock. I shut down the inboard engine and was powering the aircraft parallel to the dock when, all of a sudden, I'm heading for the rocks. Dougie had decided that the knot the roughneck tied was not good enough, and he had untied it.

The floats were banging on the rocks by the time I got the engine restarted and gained some semblance of control. Now, my diplomacy has never been a topic of a barroom table, so the language used while hollering from beyond the sandbar will be left to your imagination. Basically, I wanted Dougie off the dock and the roughneck to tie me up. I was able to get this through to Dougie, but it took a while. The end result was that the aircraft was finally secured to the dock and shut down. I figured a coffee would be in order and told Dougie to stay with the airplane while the roughneck and I went to the cook shack. It would be nice if this was the end of the story, but there's more.

The load on the airplane was a huge differential out of one of the trucks. Set in a cradle of two-by-tens, it was awkward to say the least. I had brought a barrel ramp with us to slide the differential down, but it would still require two or three men to handle it safely. For some reason that I will never know, Dougie off-loaded it by himself, well almost, that is. He managed to get it halfway down the ramp before it slipped off the side and landed upside down on the top of the float, punching through the top and putting about a six-inch hole in the back compartment. The trip back to Norman Wells was done in silence. Dougie went back to flying the 185, and I got a new crewman the next day. I'm sure it was the best way to go.

Turbo Beaver and the Engineer

From two miles back on final, I could see the Turbo Beaver taxiing about the lake in an erratic manner. Changing my landing path to avoid it, I touched down and tied up to the dock in time to watch the other aircraft rock back on its heels and launch out over the trees. Turning to the pilot of the Beaver, who was sitting on a barrel drinking not his first beer of the night, I said, "John, what's going on? Who's flying your airplane?"

"Beats me," he replied. "Must be the engineer."

"Does he know how to fly?" I asked, as we watched the airplane shudder its way around a turn.

"Doesn't look like it," John replied, downing another swallow of his beer.

We watched the plane level out on final, but when it reached the glassy water, the power went back on and the scary turns started over again. Thinking I might be able to talk him down onto the river, I climbed into the Twin Otter and tried to make contact on the radio — to no avail. All we could do was watch as attempt after attempt was aborted.

It happened that there was a big barbecue party going on at the lake, and it wasn't long before fifty to sixty people were strung out on the dock with beers and plates of food, watching this impromptu show.

Finally, on what attempt I don't know, the power was cut at about thirty feet. The plane crashed to the lake, breaking one float and driving the fuselage strut through the other one. We took a 185 that was tied to the dock and taxied out to get a line to the plane so we could tow it to shore before it sank. The pilot? The engineer climbed out onto the float, and to say he was white would be a great understatement. "I guess that wasn't much of a show," he said.

To which I replied, "Oh, I don't know. There is an awfully big audience, and no one has left." We towed him to shore and tied the aircraft in the shallows. John picked this time to tear a strip off the poor bugger. After listening to this for a minute, I stepped between them and advised the engineer that he really didn't have to take any abuse from John because chances were that he was no longer working for that company, anyway. With a few descriptive words to John, the engineer asked if he could borrow my truck.

We all returned to the party, which continued for many hours. It turned out that the engineer had just installed a new generator or alternator and was checking output. In his words, "I pushed the throttle in, looked down at my meter, and when I looked up, I was airborne. I've never been so scared in my life."

I've heard many versions of this story over the years, but this is how it was. No shit.

Figure 7. The aircraft after the hard landing

Figure 8. The aircraft after the hard landing

Competition

Kenn Borek Air had the best fleet of Otters in the Arctic and probably in the world. Equipped with excellent gear and qualified crews, it was an honour to be a *Borek Pilot*. Competition had a hard time competing with us, but they often would underbid and attempt to do work that was beyond their aircraft's ability. Rather than elaborate on this, I think the following pictures will say it all.

Figure 8a. Stuck Twin Otter

Figure 9. Stuck Twin Otter and Rescue Plane

Mayday

With a loud sharp cough, the engine stops.

Soon, the feathered prop stands still.

I'm only at two thousand feet,

Not much height for these ills.

"Mayday, Mayday." It's VVY.

The frantic cry goes out,

Transmitting blind for there's no reply,

Just hope someone's about.

I'm going down forty miles northwest

En route to the Sans Sault.

I've four on board and a load of fuel,

And nothing else will do

But find a place to set this plane,

There are no options to take,

No room for error.

If I'm to get into that little lake.

I plan my glide to turn final

Just inches off the trees.

Now, nose hard down, then pull it back,

And smack into the weeds.

We're down and safe, no damage done.

Thank God with all your might.

The passengers are all OK.

Except for one, "the fright."

We'll pole to shore and light a fire,

And make a cup of tea.

I hope that someone heard my call,

And knows just where we'll be.

The rescue plane has been and gone.

Then back again with spares.

Now, Keith and I will fix this thing.

We'll soon be in the air.

We've dumped the fuel and pumped the floats,

Got rid of excess gear.

I'm sure that we can make it now,

Though we've got some trees to clear.

I often look at that little lake

As I go out that way.

Thank God, it was an Otter

I was flying on that day.

First Trip to the High Arctic

It was spring of 1973, and I was based in Norman Wells with a Single Otter CF-CZO. I had flown the previous summer on floats, then switched to wheels and skis for the winter. It was great. The accommodation was good, the flying varied, and there was time for the odd afternoon of fishing or hunting caribou.

When Edmonton called to ask if I would be interested in a contract in the high Arctic with an ice seismic company, I readily agreed—on condition that I come back to the Wells for the summer with a Twin Otter.

Two weeks later, I left Edmonton with another Single Otter CF-CZP bound for Yellowknife, Cambridge Bay, Resolute Bay, and King Christian Island, the base for Phoenix Ventures. After an overnight in Yellowknife, I was fuelled and flight planning for Cam Bay when an older pilot, looking over my flight plan, suggested I use a nine thousand foot instead of the three-thousand-foot level that I had requested.

This was my first contact with and the start of a career-long friendship with Rocky Parsons. At the time, Rocky was one of the senior pilots with Northward Airlines and, as we discussed where I was going and the experience I had, he obviously felt I needed some help. Telling me to delay for an hour or so, he disappeared into town and returned later with a large box of survival rations and his personal gear. The box was to be tied into the front of the aircraft cabin and to stay there, no matter what. He informed me that he was on time off, but he felt that he should accompany me north. It was with some reluctance that I agreed to this plan, though within a few hours, I was more than a little happy to have him along. My experience, ability, and knowledge soon proved totally inadequate for the job ahead. As Rocky talked me through the descent and landing at Cambridge Bay, I realized I had a bunch to learn about high Arctic flying.

The fact that I had no I.F.R. time proved to be a major problem. The Astro Compass and convergence were unknown items to me and, without Rocky's input, I am sure I would still be lost somewhere between Yellowknife and Cambridge Bay. Rocky stayed with me to King Christian Island where we worked the contract and practised approaches on the small beacon. As the days went by, the head shaking changed direction from horizontal to vertical as I slowly came up to speed, and Rocky finally considered me fit to go.

I survived the season. The lessons Rocky gave me were used and added to over the years. Our paths crossed many times, and I always came away a wiser and safer pilot. Rocky and I have both retired now . We last met at a fly-in at Yellowknife in the summer of 2003. Hard to believe that thirty years has gone by. Thanks Brock.

Figure 10. Single Otter CF-CZP waiting for a weather break on King Christian Island, spring 1973

Figure 11. A better day

Single Otter

I think of days I used to fly

A Single Otter through the sky.

O'er rotting ice with wheels for gear,

And think I had nothing to fear.

From Edmonton to Resolute Bay,

With fuel stops along the way

At Cambridge Bay and Yellowknife,

I'd tell myself this is the life.

Now looking back on memories hazy,

I'm almost sure I once was crazy.

Jim

Flying a Single Otter out of Norman Wells in the early '70s was some of the most fun I ever had—long days, generally good weather, and lots of flying.

Jim McCauley, an old retired fur trader and trapper, had returned to his cabin on Good Hope Bay, on the northwest arm of Great Bear Lake, where he had lived as a young man. Whenever I had extra room and went out that way, I would drop in with some groceries or a drum of fuel and check that he was doing OK. Sometimes I was unable to stop, but if there was smoke coming from the chimney, I figured he was fine.

We spent many a delightful evening at Jim's cabin, and I will tell you about one of them as well as I can remember.

I had arranged a ride from Edmonton to Great Bear Trophy Lodge for my folks, picked them up, and flew to Jim's. After dropping them off, I returned to the Wells, turned the Otter over to maintenance for the weekend, and chartered a Cessna 185 back to Good Hope Bay. My hunting and fishing buddy Ernie Christensen and his wife, Lee, accompanied me. As it turned out, a helicopter pilot and his wife also arrived. So, we had the makings of a great weekend of fishing, cold beer, and barbecued lake trout. The long evenings turned into dusk over a few bottles of Scotch.

Figure 12. Jim's cabin. Jim is at the far right next to Lee and Ernie, who is wearing the cowboy hat.

Jim never drank when he was alone, but when guests were there; well, that was another story entirely. He didn't drink Scotch but would match us drink for drink with Drambuie, which he pulled out from under his bunk in a seemingly endless supply. About 1:00 a.m., my dad was reading aloud from a book of Scottish poetry that he had taken from a shelf by Jim's bunk, where Jim, by this time, was doing a wonderful impression of being dead— coming to life only to correct the wording, the pronunciation, or to supply a missed line to a poem. Drunk as a coot, he was still able to inject the proper word or line. A wonderful time with some great folks.

Not many years after that, the powers that be decided that Jim could not be on his own out there, and they moved him to town where he lasted only a short while. I personally think he would have lived much longer at his cabin, and he certainly would have had a better ending.

—

Mayday

It was a beautiful summer day, the type only the far north can deliver. I had spent a lazy morning cleaning my airplane, a De Havilland Single Otter CF-VVY. I had only one trip on the books—a delivery of a small load of groceries and two barrels of fuel to Sans Sault Rapids, a pipeline test site located about seventy miles north of Norman Wells along the Mackenzie river.

Georgie Moniuk, who owned and operated the Mackenzie Mountain Lodge, had her parents visiting her. This was their first trip north, and the 737 flight to the Wells was the first air travel they had experienced. Georgie had asked me if I would give them a tour of the area in the Otter, and this seemed like the perfect time. I called and told Georgie the planned departure time, then loaded and fuelled the plane, and was ready to go when they arrived about thirty minutes later. Georgie's dad, a spry sixty-five, occupied the co-pilot seat, and Georgie and her mom sat in the rear. Explaining the emergency procedures to the older couple and assuring them there was nothing to worry about, I lifted the Otter off D.O.T Lake and headed towards Sans Sault at two thousand feet. I usually used a higher altitude, but for sightseeing this was great.

I followed the river for a way, pointing out some moose and an old trapper's cabin, then turned inland to intercept the river again at Sans Sault. Although the trees were stunted, the low areas along the river were dense with scrub spruce and willows. Cruising along, enjoying the sunshine and pointing out different areas of the Mackenzie Mountains about fifty miles to the west, I was as startled as anyone when the engine coughed twice and quit. There are three little lakes along the route I was on, and, luckily, I was within gliding distance of one of them. "Mayday! Mayday!" I called into the mike as I trimmed the aircraft to the best glide speed. No answer. "VVY is going down forty miles north of Norman Wells, hoping to make a small lake ten miles west of the river." Still no reply and no more time for that. I checked the passengers for seat belts and had them remove glasses and pens from their persons, shut off electricals, and concentrated on the landing. Clear of the trees, full flap, nose down, then back, and smack into the weeds, then out into the main part of the lake.

"Great landing," the old boy grinned. I actually think he enjoyed it. Nothing but silence from the rear compartment.

"Everyone OK back there?"

"Yes, yes, I think so." From the back with such limited visibility, it must have been scary. I climbed out on the float, grabbed the ever-present paddle, and guided the plane toward a cut line and a small sandbar. Tying to shore, I helped everyone off the plane, then got a small fire going and a pot of tea brewing. The fire and tea worked wonders, and soon everyone was relaxed and as calm as if it was a Sunday picnic.

I had no way of knowing if anyone had heard my call and was considering what to do for shelter when a Twin Otter circled overhead. Talking to the crew on the radio, I advised that we were fine but needed a pick-up. They were on the way to Fort Good Hope and would return as soon as they could unload.

Two hours later, the Twin Otter had returned and taken us to Norman Wells. An engineer and I returned to the airplane, found the problem, fixed it, finished the trip, and returned to Norman Wells in time to join Georgie and her parents for a drink in Georgie's living room. "Young man, I want you to know that we will always remember our trip to the north and especially the lovely ride you took us on. It was most exciting."

"Yes," said Georgie with a wry smile. "It was most exciting."

Moving Trappers

Moving the trappers out of Fort Good Hope to the various trap lines in late fall was not one of my favourite jobs. It usually consisted of three to four full days of cramming the Otter full of all types of miscellaneous equipment from cook stoves to camp tents, snowmobiles to sleighs, barrels of fuel, hundreds of pounds of groceries, plus whatever other gear was needed to support a family of two to six for three to four months.

Once the aircraft was sitting with the rear of the floats under an inch or two of water, it was time to bring the dogs down to the dock. To dispel any romantic notion about these dog teams, let me set down a few requirements that an Indian sleigh dog must meet. One: It must be a cross of at least four types of dog that results in some long-haired, snarling beast that is at least eighteen inches at the shoulder and weighs in at between sixty and eighty pounds. Two: It must be able to survive the summer season, tied to a peg with a four-foot length of chain and fed only a fish or a piece of old moose meat once or twice a week. To be fair, these dogs, after three to four weeks in harness with a good diet and proper exercise are fine-looking animals—clean, well filled out, and weighing in at between eighty and one hundred pounds. This is not the case in the fall; they are skinny mongrels with their coats generally a solid mat of stinking brown hair, complete with a four-foot piece of chain, each link of which is plugged solid with some substance one would never consider touching with bare hands. The dogs were generally brought to the dock one at a time, and I found the best method to load them was to put the owner inside the plane, pass him the end of the chain, then grab the dog by tail and throw it in. The meaner ones usually had their heads tied down close to whatever there was to tie to. The owner usually stayed in the back with a stick to maintain order.

The load, well actually it was two trips, that sticks in my memory consisted of the usual gear, plus eight dogs and a family of four, plus a fourteen-foot canoe that had to be tied to the float of my Single Otter. Leaving the dogs and the canoe for the second trip (this proved to be a big mistake), we loaded the camp gear, groceries, and passengers and flew to a small lake about a hundred miles away where we parked on the bottom about fifty feet from shore.

For the next three hours, we packed supplies through the frigid water to the campsite. The last load, with a little girl around six on my shoulders, was about all I could manage. Cold and wet, the father and I climbed back into the aircraft and returned to Fort Good Hope for the second load. After the dogs were on board and the remaining gear was loaded, we were tying the canoe to the struts when Joe looked me in the eye and said, "We shoulda taken the canoe on the first trip." Why he waited 'till then to say something, I will never know. We flew back to his camp, threw his dogs into the lake, loaded the remaining freight into the canoe, and I left— thankful that this was the last load, and that in a couple of hours I would be home in Norman Wells, warm and dry.

I thought no more of Joe until he appeared on the dock at Fort Good Hope the following spring. "Hey Pilot, you remember last fall you took me out to my trapline?"

"Yes" I replied, trying to place him.

"You remember you threw my dogs into the lake?"

Oh yes, that narrowed it down to about ten.

"Well, my best dog, he run into the bush and got his chain caught and choked hisself. What are you going to do about that? He was a hundred-dollar dog."

"Augh." I almost choked on that one myself. "I'm sorry about that but these things happen, and I can't do anything about it."

"And you guys charged me ten dollars extra for hauling my canoe. What you going to do about that?"

"I can't do anything about that either." I explained that the extra charge was for the time spent tying and untying the boat, plus the slower airspeed used with an external load.

"But that canoe was for your convenience."

"My convenience?"

"Sure, you know that lake is too shallow to get to the shore. What you gonna do, throw my stuff in the water?"

A bit of an addition to this story: Twenty-some years later, I was doing a shift in Inuvik and was in the bar one evening with some friends when a lovely young woman came and sat beside me. "Hey Pilot," she laughed." Do you remember me? You carried me to shore to my father's camp when I was a little girl. My father is dead now, but I still remember that. We had many laughs around the campfire about the canoe. And, by the way, that dog was not a good dog, anyways."

Figure 13. Otter load of frozen Caribou from one of the winter camps

Flying for a Major Oil Company

I was approached by the chief pilot for Gulf Oil in late 1974 to join their Twin Otter crew doing support for their drilling operation in the Mackenzie Delta. These jobs were the cream of the industry with excellent aircraft and maintenance, two-week rotations, high salary, and loads of company benefits. I jumped at the chance. Little did I realize how much I would miss the float flying that I had been doing for the previous years.

I lasted just over two years; the boredom of the short, repetitive flights between rigs situated sometimes less that ten miles apart was more than I could take. So, when Gulf cut back on their crew requirements, I was more than happy to move on.

The chief pilot of Kenn Borek Air called two days later and offered me a choice of flying out of Inuvik or Resolute Bay in the high Arctic Islands. I chose Resolute Bay and spent some happy years doing some very challenging flying. I loved the off-strip work with large, low-pressure, high-flotation tires, and the ski work on the ocean ice during the twenty-four-hour daylight season. In the twenty-four-hour nights, I flew support for drilling activity, medivacs, and scheduled flights to communities across the north.

Temperatures into the minus 50s and lots of wind and snow gave me the experience I needed later on for Antarctica. But before I get too far ahead of myself—a few more poems of the Arctic.

Pilot's Dream

Tonight's the type of night I love,

Rig lights below, the stars above,

A big round moon to light my way,

The snow below as bright as day,

Beacon signals loud and clear,

Why can't it stay like this all year?

Instead of nights as black as pitch

That really make your back hairs itch.

Descending through a dark black hole

Without a trace of light below.

Perhaps a glimpse of runway lights,

Too late, back up into the night.

Easy Money

I'm right down in the clag tonight.

There's no light to be seen.

It's socked in tight where I'm to go,

And also where I've been.

Air radio advises that

All stations, far and near,

Are deteriorating rapidly.

Now that, I hate to hear.

I've shot I.L.S. approaches

And ridden down the beam,

To limits minus fifty,

But no ground have I seen.

My landing lights just flare right back,

It's like a wall of white.

So, leave them off and strain to see

Into the darkest night.

The forecasters were calling for

More than four hundred feet,

With vis of two or maybe three,

In blowing snow and sleet.

Now I'm not sure how far ahead

These eyes of mine can see.

But much below four hundred feet,

I sure don't want to be.

I climb to seven thousand

Where the moon and stars are bright.

While down below, those ice-filled clouds

Are causing me a fright.

My fuel is down to bare reserves.

It won't be very long,

Before I get a warning light

To tell me that it's gone.

It's times like this I ask myself,

What am I doing here?

I could be home with wife and kids,

And have nothing to fear.

I guess the only thing to do

Is make a final try

At slipping down the glide slope,

A case of do or die.

I hit the outer marker

At minimums, then less.

I whisper, help me out, oh God,

'Cause I'm sure in a mess.

And then, below my wingtip,

At fifty feet, no more,

The runway lights are passing,

My mind lets out a roar.

Slam it on and full reverse,

Don't worry 'bout finesse.

How deep-gut scared you really were,

No one must ever guess.

So, shut it down and get some sleep.

Today you earned your pay.

You *easy money* pilot,

At least that's what they say.

Medivac

Midnight call out, Medivac,

It's fifty-six below.

The Arctic winds are at their best,

A thirty-five-knot blow.

Down the strip, I see three lights,

The ceiling is unknown.

While in the back, the stretcher case

Continues painful moans.

The sharp gusts slap at the controls

During my brief run up.

I hope that it's just ground effect,

And smooths off higher up.

Now off the strip, retract the flaps,

And right into the clag,

At fifty feet, the lights are gone,

Are we in for a ride.

We're tossed and bucked, it's rough as hell,

Up to two thousand feet.

But now, it smooths and starts to clear

As through the tops we creep.

Inuvik strip is calling clear

With gusts to thirty-eight.

Straight down the strip from two two o,

Now that's a pleasant break.

We're by Noel and out of three,

"Call right base twenty-two."

"You're number one," then

"Cleared to land." "Roger, check, thank you"

The ambulance is waiting,

And they're quickly on their way.

While I have yet to bed the bird,

For here I'll have to stay.

I'll catch a nap on an airport bench,

But every hour or so,

I'll have to fire the engines up,

For it's fifty-six below.

I think about my warmed-up bunk,

I left one hour ago,

And wish to hell I was still there,

And Bob had had to go.

Guyana

The short, narrow, concrete runway seemed to float in the midst of the flooded rice paddies as we descended on the final leg of our flight from Canada to British Guyana on the northeast corner of South America. The heat, humidity, and rank smell of rotting vegetation hit us like a wall as we taxied in and parked the aircraft for the night.

Years of operating in the Canadian Arctic had certainly not prepared us for the high temperatures or the abundance of bugs, snakes, 'gators, and other swamp-type creatures that we would meet over the life of this contract. The Kaboura fly, the equivalent of the Canadian black fly, caused blood to run freely and was about the only insect we could relate to.

We arrived at the airstrip the next morning about 10:00 with temperatures already pushing 30°C. The night guard couldn't wait to show us the alligator that he had killed beside the airplane during the night. That, my engineer informed me, puts an end to any thoughts of doing night maintenance. "Can you imagine backing down the ladder in the dark and stepping into that?"

Figure 14. The alligator shot beside our airplane the first night we were in Guyana

We were soaked with sweat by the time we had off-loaded the ferry equipment and were ready to take our first flight. The heat waves coming off the runway turned the concrete to a pool of glistening water a few hundred feet in front of the plane as I lined up for takeoff. Using a paper towel to wipe the sweat from my eyes and glasses, I started the takeoff roll while monitoring the gauges closely for temperatures. Glancing at the airspeed indicator as the needle approached sixty knots, the needle

disappeared from sight. With the runway nearly all behind us at this point, we had to fly, and as I rotated, something flew off the dash and stuck to my bare chest between my open shirt lapels. I grabbed at this thing and threw it into the back of the plane as we wobbled out over the rice paddies. As we climbed to a safer altitude and my heart rate descended toward normal, the engineer pointed out the small tree frog that was sticking to the ceiling in the cabin of the aircraft. It had obviously been stuck to the glass of the airspeed indicator then moved to my chest at about the worst time it could have picked.

Guyana Airport Terminal

In 1981, we started a contract in Georgetown, Guyana, flying support for a drilling operation. The contract called for a pilot and engineer, and we were to use a local air force pilot as a co-pilot. This did not work out all that well because the air force pilots were used to having a bunch of people do the actual work involved. At the end of the day, Billy my engineer and I would be sweat-stained and dirty while the assigned co-pilot would be as clean and fresh as when the day started. It also didn't seem to matter whether the pilots were actually flying or doing the paperwork, you could look across and often they would be sound asleep.

This contract was for a Canadian oil company that was drilling a well in southern Guyana. Our rotation was every three weeks, and the flights in and out of the country could be exasperating. It was not the worst airport we had ever worked out of, but it was close. There were two airlines servicing it from the States, each with two flights a week. Both arrived at the same time, and the terminal was hard-pressed to handle the one to two hundred people that arrived about 10:00 p.m. If the Guyana President's plane arrived at the same time, we were forced to stay on board with the windows covered until he had departed the airport.

Our crew of two, plus a few oil workers, were the only white faces in the crowd of people pushing their way through to the customs and immigration personnel. Standing in line with temperatures in the 90-100°F range was brutal, and the fact that we were held back while everyone around us was processed was exasperating, to say the least. Two to three hours later, we would step out into the hot, humid darkness, often to find only one dilapidated taxi available. Something had to change.

I talked with the supervisors of the oil company we were working for and got the OK to do a P.R. flight to our rig and the camp about two hundred miles away. Inviting the head of immigration, the head of customs, and the airport manager to visit the rig and join us for a meal at the camp was the best thing I could have done. The next crew to arrive was personally escorted through the crowds and was first out the door. Three weeks later, when Billy and I arrived, we were called to the front of the line. "Captain Harry, Billy, welcome back." With a few small gifts throughout the contract, we were never again pushed to the back of the line.

A Very Dry Trip

Billy and I were on our way from Guyana to Calgary on our regular three-week rotation. The airline we used from Guyana to New York always treated us very well, and we were generally upgraded to first class. However, on this trip, the first class had been sold out and we were in the economy section. We were still given the first-class treatment concerning drinks and meals, so it really wasn't that much of a hardship. The first-class service consisted of a bottle of whatever you drank, and the flight attendants kept you supplied with ice and mix. The four-plus hour flight passed quickly and, except for the two children behind us who kept kicking the seats and slamming the trays up and down, everything went well.

Arriving in New York, we had a two-hour wait for the Air Canada flight to Calgary, so, of course, we went to the bar for a few more drinks. There seemed to be an excess number of children on the flight to Calgary, and, after we levelled off and had been served a drink, the thoughts of having two misbehaved kids sitting behind us again on this leg was not pleasant. When the flight attendant stopped by our seats to advise us that they were going to feed all the children first and would then start the meal service, Billy looked up at her and said, "That's a really great idea. Why don't you feed them all to the f---ing alligators." Need I say, we never did get another drink on that trip.

A Scary Night

Kenn Borek Air had bought a new Twin Otter for a contract in South America and installed an air-conditioning system in it. It had never worked properly, and one night it finally decided to quit.

I was flying for a Canadian oil company based in Georgetown, Guyana. The aircraft was a beautiful new Twin Otter painted in the oil company's colours. Well equipped with Weather Radar and many extras, it was a joy to fly. I got a call one afternoon to fly to Trinidad and pick up four barrels of acid that was needed at the rig. Acid is something we are not supposed to fly, but there was a lot of pressure from the rig boss and I thought it would work out.

We departed Trinidad about two a.m. and headed for Georgetown about six hundred miles away. Climbing through eight thousand feet, the engineer came forward to tell me that the acid was seeping up through the bungs of two of the barrels. He had used paper towels and some rags to keep it sopped up and contained on the tops of the barrels. Not too big a problem yet. I called Georgetown and requested clearance to proceed direct to the rig site and put on the air conditioning to cool things down and hopefully slow the seepage.

The coastline of Venezuela was coming up ahead of us and, though we were not supposed to go into their airspace, I cut across a corner to shorten the flight time. Ahead of us was one of the biggest lightening storms I have ever seen. A towering cumulonimbus cloud was lighting up from the ground to at least thirty thousand feet, every few minutes. With the radar painting a solid red mass ahead, we had to deviate about thirty miles to get around it. It was then that the air-conditioning unit decided to quit and did so by burning the insulation off some of its wiring and putting a lot of smoke into the cockpit. Coupled with the fumes from the acid, this was not a nice place to be.

Now Billy comes forward again, saying he is out of rags and paper towel and has used his shirt and pants, but needs more. I gave him my shirt and sent the co-pilot back to help him. Finally, we got past the storm and were able to start descent into the rig. The radio operator advised us that a couple of customs agents were waiting for us at the strip, but he wasn't sure why. Neither was I, and we contemplated throwing the case of cigarettes and case of Scotch that we had bought in Trinidad out the back door. We finally decided to stash them in the far rear of the aircraft and made much to do about getting the barrels off the plane. That, coupled with a half-naked aircrew, worked, and the inspectors never even got on the airplane. They were concerned that we had not returned via Georgetown, but with all the troubles we were having, they waved it off. Would I do that again? NO WAY.

Guyana, South America

I was flying support for a Canadian oil company drilling for oil close to the Brazilian border. Due to the shortage of supplies in Guyana, we would fly into Boa Vista, Brazil, at least once a week.

Figure 15. C-GKBG in British Guyana

The airport at Boa Vista, Brazil, was clean and modern; the only shortage seemed to be English-speaking traffic controllers—not an uncommon situation in the smaller centres around the world. While not a big problem usually, it was the cause of some amusing incidents. First off, let me explain that Brazilian Civil Aviation forbids night flying of aircraft with fewer than three engines. Airlines operating on airways are excluded from this restriction, but the Twin Otter I was flying had to be clear of Brazilian airspace before it was officially dark.

On the apron, with the engines running, I called for departure clearance. Inside the tower, the normal procedures were put on hold while everyone began the search for the only English speaker on staff. It was not unusual for this to take ten minutes or so, but as the time crept by and my departure time that would enable me to clear Brazil's border before dark got closer, I called again asking for taxi and departure clearance. I guess the English speaker was unavailable because the reply came back with a strong Portuguese accent "kilo-bravo-golfea, go away, go away" With tears of laughter running down our cheeks, we taxied and departed. "Buenos noches amigos."

Fishing in Guyana

Just so you don't think flying is all work, here is a short fishing story from Guyana. I had picked up the director of Civil Aviation and his wife in Georgetown and flown out to a small ranching operation close to the Brazilian border. After securing the airplane and having lunch, or rather, tea, with the mother and daughter team that owned the property, we crawled into two small dugout boats about twelve feet long with a freeboard of maybe three inches and paddled up a narrow jungle river.

Figure 16. Jungle river

Talk about a Tarzan movie! There were thick vines to duck under and weave through and alligators sliding down the banks to disappear in the brown water as we approached. After a few miles of this, the river widened into a small lake where we were to fish. Casting towards the shore, we soon had a number of beautifully coloured fish of about four to six pounds. Called Lukanani, they proved a great eating fish, and we had quite a feast that night.

But let me get back to the story. After removing a fish from my line, I flipped my hook out towards the deep water and immediately had a fish on. Our guide, in broken English, let me know in no uncertain terms that that was a mistake, and I watched as he beat the fish off the hook and would not even bring it into the boat. "Piranha very bad fish," he explained. After considerable negotiation, he consented to let me catch one to bring back to the airplane where my camera waited. When I brought this fish to the side of the boat, the guide carefully lifted it in, then drove his knife through it and into the side of the boat. On the way back down the river, the guide turned to me and explained his thoughts on piranha. "Lukanani fish, flip-flop, flip-flop, no problem. Piranha fish, flip-flop, flip-flop, no toe."

Figure 17. Black piranha about twelve inches long

Figure 18. Lukanani

Belugas and Young

One of the great things about flying a Twin Otter was the ability to enjoy wonders like this. The Belugas come into the warmer shallow waters along the coast of Somerset Island to give birth to their young. After taking this picture, I landed and walked to the shoreline. It was awesome watching and listening to the whales passing within feet of where I sat.

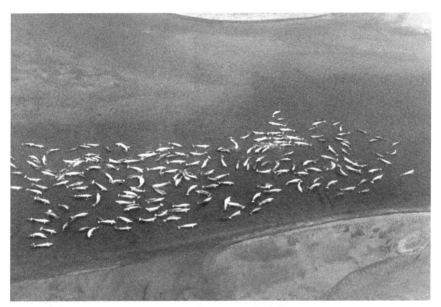

Figure 19. Beluga whales with young at Somerset Island, Nunavut.

Friends

I think of my friends in the Arctic,

And I think how poor it would be,

If a man had no one to talk to,

And no one to share his whisky.

And I think of the times I've been asked in to dine,

Though the meal was just simple fare.

A Caribou stew means much more with you,

Than a T-bone with those who don't care.

It sure gives a man a warm feeling,

To have a few friends such as you,

A place where you always feel welcome,

And never explaining to do.

A real northern friend just accepts you,

Face value with no questions asked,

For the haves and the have-nots don't matter,

When a true northern friendship is cast.

You Think You're Alone

It's 2:00 in the morning and the summer sun of the Canadian Arctic is casting long shadows down the fiords and across the still waters of the lakes, creating silver mirrors in the barren landscape. Times like this, you can get to thinking you are the only person in the world. I'm sure that's what the pilot of the Single Otter was thinking as he called up six nine Resolute on the H.F. radio and passed the message to dispatch that he was landing at the camp and would be shutting down for a few hours sleep. The person working dispatch just happened to be his girlfriend, and the closing of his transmission went something like this, "That's it for tonight, darling. I'll see you in the morning. Kiss, kiss. Good night." Well, you are never alone on H.F., and so from polar routing 747s and helicopters working the mainland barrens came at least a dozen kiss, kiss, good nights.

Get Rich Quick

I guess everyone has had a get rich scheme or two, something that looked to be a certain money-maker with little or no risk. Matt the co-pilot and I were cruising along one day north of Resolute Bay when we tuned in the coastguard frequency and heard that a large cruise ship was diverting into Grise Fiord for a one-day stop. The arrival time was late the next day, and we had a charter into Grise early that same morning.

Dealing with the manager of the northern store in Resolute, we *borrowed* all his carvings and spent hours there repricing, wrapping, and packing the carvings to take to Grise the next morning. Leaving a few hours early allowed us time to unpack and arrange the carvings on a display rack that we had borrowed from the local co-op.

Departing Grise with our charter, the fog bank and ice flow to the east of Coburg Island did little to dampen the thoughts of our eminent windfall. Two days later with Grise Fiord still zero-zero in fog, the cruise ship pulled out without ever getting a passenger to shore. To add insult to injury, while we were packing up the carvings the following week to return them to Resolute, one of the larger pieces was found to be broken. Of course, no one could imagine how that could have happened.

I took the piece to a local carver I knew, who repaired the carving for a small price, though it remained somewhat distorted, and the store manager in Resolute agreed to overlook the disfigurement in exchange for a bottle of black rum.

The total cost of this fiasco:

- $40.00 for the carver

- $40.00 for the rum

- Six hours labour for the packing and pricing

  Cheap compared to a few other schemes we had.

Worst Christmas Ever

Ernie and I had been rotating shifts opposite each other for some time, but we had never really spent any time together and, in fact, hardly knew each other. Ernie was going to be in Resolute Bay over Christmas and New Year's, and he phoned me in Resolute to tell me he was coming up a week early, so I could get home to do the pre-Christmas things with my family. Two days after we rotated, the company did an aircraft switch, sending a plane out of Calgary to Resolute and bringing the base aircraft south for maintenance.

It was December 21, 1977: The crew for the ferry flight spent most of the morning in Resolute and departed for Calgary about the same time Ernie was leaving for the scheduled flight to Nanisivik and Pond Inlet. On the return leg, on approach to Nanisivik, the aircraft had a flap rod failure and crashed short of the runway, killing the crew and six passengers. There were, I believe six such failures before the manufacturer admitted to the problem and came up with a fix.

The southbound aircraft had reached Yellowknife, but the crew refused to return to Resolute, saying the navigation equipment was not good enough to do the flight. Remember this was long before G.P.S. was available. The company phoned me at home and asked if I could meet up with a Lear jet that they were chartering to fly to the crash site. They would drop me at Yellowknife to take the Otter back north.

The Lear dropped me off at about 2:00 a.m. and it was cold, -40°, but no wind. I located the Otter to find it cold-soaked, not plugged in, not unloaded, not fuelled, and no one around. The aircraft did start (just), and I spent an hour unloading it. Then I loaded six empty drums on board and contacted the fuel man. Three hours after I arrived, I was finally flight planning for the trip north. About this time, the co-pilot of the ferry crew showed up and offered to come with me. "You knew how this was going to happen, yet you and that asshole captain couldn't even unload and fuel this aircraft? Now you want to come with me? I don't want anything to do with you, and you can tell your captain that the same goes for him."

I landed at Cambridge Bay for fuel and a weather forecast for Resolute Bay. It wasn't good, but with the fuel I had on board, I could shoot approaches for an hour and still go to Rae Point, about two hundred miles west, if I didn't get in.

About a hundred miles north of Cam Bay, I got a call to return to Cambridge. Thinking that the Lear had not been able to get into Nanisivik, I turned back and asked what time the Lear was estimating. "We have no Lear traffic inbound," was the reply.

"Then where did this return to Cam Bay message come from?"

"It came from your base manager in Resolute, he says the weather is too bad, and you are to wait in Cambridge."

"Roger. Check that. I am setting course for Resolute Bay, and the revised estimate is 19:30.

Arriving overhead Resolute, the radio operator was less than helpful and threatened me with a violation if I attempted to land. Well, a radio operator is not a controller and has no say in what weather conditions a plane might land. Blowing snow caused by the high easterly winds reduced visibility to next to nothing on the ground, but from above you could see down through it. It would be only the last forty feet or so that would be tricky. I was planning on using the cross-strip but requested that the high-intensity lighting for the main strip be left on until I was established on final. Then, when I called, the operator was to switch the cross-strip lights on. I had explained this clearly, but when I called for the switch for the lights, I got a reply "Say again."

"Wow," I thought, "this guy is not going to help me at all."

Back up into the night, and again I try to get set up for the cross-strip. It took three tries to get down, and then I had to get a truck to come out and guide me into the ramp.

December 23: One of the worst trips I ever had to do. I flew from Resolute Bay to Nanisivik, flying over the remains of the wrecked Otter on approach. I loaded six coffins and proceeded to Pond Inlet where the terminal was packed with family and friends of the deceased. It seemed to take forever to get off-loaded and away from the sounds of screaming, crying children and wailing adults. From there, I had to go back to Nanisivik, load the coffins of our two crewmen and return them to Resolute. All the while, in the back of my mind, was the thought that if Ernie had not come back a week early, it would be me in the back of the plane.

December 24: We got word from Nanisivik airport that a large shipment of Christmas mail for Pond Inlet had arrived that afternoon. I contacted the Nanisivik airport manager, who I knew quite well, and arranged for him to open the airport, so I could pick up this mail. I thought that, in some small way, this might make Christmas in Pond Inlet a bit more bearable. Unloading in Pond about midnight, a man I knew came up to the aircraft, telling me that he was unable to get home to his family in Grise Fiord for Christmas. I had nothing on the books over Christmas, and Christmas Day in Grise Fiord with some friends of mine would be as much fun as in Resolute. "Get in. I'm probably in trouble anyway, what's a bit more?" It

---

was almost 3:00 a.m. when I landed at Grise Fiord, and by the time I had the plane blanketed, plugged in and had walked down the hill, there were no lights at the settlement manager's house or the R.C.M.P. house where I usually stayed. I opened the door to the jail and found some blankets for the bunk in cell one, my usual spot when things were crowded. I was looking forward to the Christmas meal at the community hall the next day when the call came in to do a medivac to Eureka, a remote weather station north of Grise Fiord. Well, that put the kibosh on any Christmas plans I had, so I tracked down the fuel truck driver and headed out to Eureka. By the time I got back to Resolute, there was nothing but bones left from the turkey and the party was long over. This was a far cry from the family Christmas I had planned only ten short days before.

Oh yes: The medivac patient. Turns out all he had was a bellyache, and by the time the nurses in Resolute saw him, he was ready to go back to work.

Ice Landings

I was fortunate to work with the Institute of Ocean Sciences for two seasons: installing strings of data gathering equipment that were attached to the ocean floor under the Arctic ice one year, then locating and recovering them the next year. This work required many ice landings and gave me time to wander around from ice pan to ice pan, drilling holes to determine ice thickness.

Figure 20. Removing an ice core to allow equipment to be lowered to the ocean floor

By the time I started doing North Pole trips in 1978, I was quite confident that I could estimate the ice conditions on the many refrozen leads that develop with the constantly shifting ice between northern Ellesmere Island and the North Pole. Different shades of white indicated different thicknesses and that, backed up by subsequent drifting patterns, ensured that there was sufficient thickness to support the aircraft. Thankfully, this experience prevented me from being involved in any circumstance like those shown in the following pictures.

Figure 21. An aircraft shortly after coming to a stop at the North Pole. Luckily, all the passengers were able to exit through the pilot's door. The main doors were unusable. Also, very luckily, the radios worked, so an emergency message could be passed.

Figure 22. The aircraft a short time later as it settled down to the wings. Within a few hours, the aircraft nosed down and began its final descent to the minus ten-thousand-foot level. No one was injured, and the rescue plane arrived prior to anyone getting seriously cold.

Hot Air Balloon

Sail a hot air balloon over the North Pole? "Sure, why not?" I shrugged and walked away, filing this idea with the many other oddball schemes I had been approached with. Since successfully supplying air support for a solo dogsled trip to the Pole in 1978, it seemed everyone had some crazy notion.

I had completely forgotten the idea when I arrived back in Resolute Bay after three weeks south. "The balloonists will be here on Saturday," Tom Frook, our base manager advised me. "How are you managing the logistics for this one?"

No small question that, as each North Pole trip required meticulous planning for fuel, fuel caches on the ice, equipment, food, and personnel for our base camp at Lake Hazen. Opening the camp, in itself, was a big job. Lake Hazen is located 640 miles north of Resolute and 567 miles south of the Pole. It would take two or three flights with fuel, food, and some labour to shovel out and heat up the Parkalls, then get a water supply from the river, hook up propane, and connect fuel barrels to the oil heaters.

Lake Hazen to the Pole consists of ninety miles of rugged mountain range that reaches up to 8,500 feet, then 477 miles of rough, broken sea ice intersected by numerous open leads. The distance requires a fuel cache placed about 350 miles out and while you might think that five fuel barrels would be easy enough to find on a white background, such is not always the case. Shifting and moving, the ice surface can change a smooth landing area to a broken mess in a matter of hours. If weather delays are encountered, the ice could move fifteen to twenty miles over a few days. A lost cache would cost in excess of $10,000.00 plus the time, which is even more valuable.

Meeting with the balloon crew on their arrival at Resolute, I still had many doubts about the sanity and feasibility of this venture. Talking with the crew as we went over the equipment that was required, I was impressed with the no-nonsense attitude and with the lack of extras that usually plague a trip of this nature. "Looks good, let's do it."

Having covered the weight allowance and fuel caching problems, the briefing moved to weather, the deciding, yet most unpredictable, factor in a successful mission. Past experience had shown high Arctic weather forecasts to be unreliable, to say the least. A single open lead in the wrong place can create a fog bank that extends for miles.

The weather at Hazen must be good and indicated to stay that way because fuel reserves on the return trip will be minimum for both the cache and the Pole trip. Weather conditions at the cache must be good for the initial landing there, and the Pole itself had to be relatively clear to ensure that we could find a suitable landing area in this world of white. Winds must be light enough to eliminate blowing snow, and, in this case, lighter still to ensure a safe flight for the balloon crew. I went on to explain that the initial plan of drifting over the Pole and being picked up at a different location would not be acceptable due to the difficulty of finding suitable landing areas, a fact not readily agreed on until the ice conditions were actually observed.

Good weather out of Resolute Bay and with a short fuelling stop at Grise Fiord, Canada's northernmost community, we continued on the scenic flight to the northern end of Ellesmere Island and Lake Hazen.

Stopping for a few hours sleep, I departed with the fuel cache while the balloonists did a short, but picturesque, flight along the lake.

Flying above a solid overcast layer from the coastline north towards the fuel cache area, things did not look too promising. Two hundred and fifty miles out, the sea ice began to show through breaks in the cloud. I located a suitable landing area, rolled out five barrels of fuel, then marked out a strip using green garbage bags filled with snow. Returning to Lake Hazen, the weather had moved inland and a heavy ice-crystal, ice-fog combination blanketed the area, limiting forward visibility to about half a mile. Fortunately, Ruggles River, which runs out of the lake, does so with such velocity that it stays open year-round. Using this black line as a reference, I descended, then happily landed at the camp.

The weather had cleared considerably by next morning, twenty-four-hour sunshine this time of year. And amidst good luck wishes from the camp crew, we departed. Climbing through the four-thousand-foot overcast into the bright sunshine and mountain peaks, I set course for the fuel cache 350 miles to the north. Two hours later, still above a solid overcast, I started descent. Cloud tops at twenty-four-hundred feet, I continued down to six hundred feet, where broken ice ridges gradually became visible. At three hundred feet, visibility improved to between four and five miles as we searched the ice for the five barrels. My eagle-eyed partner tapped my shoulder and pointed to the right. A few minutes later, I touched down beside the cache—thankful that I had taken the time to mark out the strip the day before. A brisk wind, coupled with the -30°C temperature kept the passengers close by while we refuelled, and no time was wasted getting airborne again.

If the light conditions were like this at the Pole, we would be unable to land. If the wind conditions were like this, the balloon would be unable to fly due mainly to the restriction I had given them: they must be able to walk back to the aircraft. We push north with fingers crossed.

Someone in the group must live right! Sixty miles from the Pole, the clouds stopped as if cut by a knife and the ice ridges sparkled blue and white below us. Ice fog drifted slowly over the open leads, indicating nearly calm winds.

At ninety degrees north, a long, curving, refrozen lead stretched south below us and, after a couple of passes to ensure suitability for landing and wind direction for the balloon, I landed. Then I retracted the skis when I found only two inches of snow on the ice. The V.L.F. Omega Navigation System showed 90° north. We were not close to the Pole, but right on it!

I could almost feel the relief and happiness of the balloon team. The delays, uncertainty, and dependence on others was over; it was now their ballgame. Perhaps I had painted too black a picture when explaining the possible problems of completing this trip. Enough of that, we were there, the weather was perfect, and all systems were go.

In the time it took to pump two barrels of fuel into the aircraft, the balloon was rolled out, the gondola assembled and attached, and inflation well underway. Unlike many ventures of this type, the balloon crew had been well organized from the start, and things proceeded without a hitch.

Very impressive—a small, caged propeller was used with a gas motor to force cold air into the balloon; then, with a couple of short bursts from the propane burner, the bag fills to about six stories high; then, it strains against the gondola, which is tethered to the ice until everything is ready. I find it hard to believe that this huge balloon will fold down and again go into the aircraft.

Figure 23. The hot air balloon towers over the Twin Otter at the North Pole.

Talking to Resolute on the H.F., they advise that Hazen has cleared and is forecast to stay that way for at least twenty-four hours. Double-checking fuel quantity showed that I had enough to do a circuit with the photographers, so they could get a shot of the balloon as it sails over the marker that we had placed on the ice.

Figure 24. The hot air balloon drifts over our North Pole marker.

Within three hours, the flight had been made, the frozen champagne toast had been made, the balloon and equipment were reloaded, and the aircraft was airborne and starting to warm up enough to remove parkas and down-filled pants on our return flight to Lake Hazen.

"Sail a hot air balloon over the Pole?"

"Sure, why not?"

Alexandra Fiord

It was a beautiful sunny day along the east coast of Ellesmere Island as we descended into Alexandra Fiord with a load of fuel in barrels for the helicopter that was working out of there. Alex Fiord is an abandoned R.C.M.P. post, used occasionally now by a handful of scientists during the summer months. There was a short Twin-Otter-only strip there, and we used it only when the winds were fairly light. This day was perfect, and we were looking forward to unloading and spending some time wandering around.

That was not to be. As we touched down, the co-pilot selected flaps up, a normal short-field procedure. Seconds later, the right tundra tire blew out, and the landing was aborted. Struggling to get airborne, the aircraft drifted off to the left of the strip, toward a row of empty fuel barrels that we were going to pick up. While lifting the left wheel slightly to miss the barrels, there was a loud bang, and the aircraft started a steep right turn. The ailerons were locked in this position, and things looked pretty bad as we circled out over a sea of huge rocks and a mountain slope. As the flaps continued to come up, the controls slowly responded to the panic-driven pressure on them, and we were able to get levelled out.

The helicopter pilot radioed us that the wing tip and a few other parts were scattered on the ridge at the end of the strip. Once we had gained some altitude and had things under control, I sent the co-pilot back to have a look out the windows and see what we had going on. He returned, looking very pale, and advised me that there was about four feet of aileron sticking straight up in the air, and the outboard hanger was totally gone.

With no decent runway to land on in the area, we set course for Eureka, one of the high Arctic weather stations, which was about 150 miles away. Eureka's weather was clear with a ten-knot crosswind coming from the north. Everything seemed to be going quite well until we reduced speed for the approach and found that, as the aircraft slowed down, the aileron control became stiffer and stiffer. Aileron control is a major factor in a cross-wind landing, and things rapidly got worse as we slowed down. Without the flat tire, we could have landed at a higher speed, but knowing we would unable to control things once we touched down added to the misery.

The end result? The aircraft sitting ninety degrees to the runway with both main tires flat and a deep gouge in the runway on the right side. The second tire had peeled off the rim when the aircraft slewed to the right.

I think luck was totally the saving factor in this incident.

It added a few grey hairs, that's for sure.

An Impromptu Wake

Tom, the base manager for Kenn Borek Air, and I were sitting in our office in the Resolute Bay Airport, waiting for the Transair flight out of Winnipeg. It had been due about 11:00 p.m., but it was now nearly 1:00 a.m. Sipping on a bottle of Scotch and discussing our flights for tomorrow helped the time go by. There was one pallet of freight and one passenger waiting for the flight.

Tom gave me a nudge and commented that the passenger, sitting across the waiting room, didn't look very good. He was a cook off one of the Canadian icebreakers that had passed Resolute earlier in the day. The helicopter that had brought him in would come back later to pick up his replacement.

Well, the weather conditions worsened and, about an hour later, the Transair flight was cancelled. Tom commented that the cook looked even worse than he had earlier. We went over to ask if he wanted to come to our complex to wait. Tom gave him a shake, and the guy fell over in the chair, dead.

This was going to make a long night because we now had to find the R.C.M.P. officer to confirm and record all this. Long story short, we did all that was required: put the guy on a stretcher, covered him up, and moved the body to the curling rink, where it sat on the ice, waiting for the next Transair flight.

The following evening, we were in the Arctic Circle Club having a few drinks when Tom decides that this poor guy probably didn't have many friends and that we should go over and have a few drinks with him. Half an hour later, there were five of us sitting along the edge of the single ice sheet, proposing toasts and wishing him well. This was Friday night and we had a bonspiel planned for Saturday evening. No problem we decided, we would just set him outside beside the curling rink until we were done.

That worked fine except, by the time the bonspiel was over, a vicious northern storm had moved in, and it was all we could do to get back to the complex. The next morning things had improved, and we went back to the curling rink. We probed down through the drifts until we located the stretcher, shovelled it out, and moved it back inside.

A Similar Story

An elderly native man from Gjoa Haven, a small Inuit community west of Cambridge Bay, had passed away in Montreal. His coffin was put on a Nordair flight headed to Frobisher Bay, now Iqaluit, then on to Resolute Bay. From Resolute, it would go via Pacific Western to Cambridge Bay, then over to Gjoa Haven. Resolute weather forced cancellation of that leg of the flight, and the coffin ended up sitting on the freight dock in Frobisher for the better part of a week before moving on to Resolute.

The spring sun can be very warm in Frobisher, and whether it was rain water or what, I don't know. But when the coffin arrived in Resolute, it was wet. Pacific Western refused to haul it without what is known as an over casket. This would have to come from Edmonton, and another week would go by.

During this time, we got a call for a DC-3 charter from Resolute to Gjoa Haven for a government group that was travelling to the Arctic communities. Tom woke me up in the middle of the night with a plan that he needed my help with. The two of us loaded the coffin into the DC-3, crammed it into the bathroom, nearly vertical, locked the bathroom door, and put an out-of-service sign on the door. We hung a curtain behind the rear seats and tied a honey bucket to the wall. The passengers had no problem with this— in those days, nearly all communities used honey buckets, so it was not much of an imposition.

Giving the bathroom key to the aircrew, we instructed them to remain on the strip at Gjoa until all the charter people had been taken to town. We would then contact our agent and tell him there was some freight on the airplane that he had to pick up.

This was one of Tom's ideas that did work out.

There were others, of course....

Rescuing the R.C.M.P. Otter at Alexandra Fiord

The R.C.M.P. operate Twin Otters around the Arctic but, for some unknown reason, have never felt it necessary to have a set of wheel skis, which would ensure that they could operate safely in the winter conditions we encounter across the north.

We got a call from the officer at Grise Fiord one early spring day, asking if we could bring a few people with shovels, pick him and a few more people up, and fly them to Alexandra Fiord. The Mounties Twin Otter on wheels had landed in some deep snow and was unable to take off.

When we arrived, we found the aircraft sitting at the end of three very deep ruts and unable to move. It took many hours of work by ten to twelve of us to hand shovel a strip that the pilot figured would be suitable. I think he was spooked, as he insisted the strip be taken down to bare ice and to what I thought was nearly twice the length and width needed.

Usually a couple bottles of Scotch would show up later for this type of effort because this sort of thing was never billed out. Not this time; I don't even remember getting a thank-you note.

Figure 25. Shovelled down to bare ice, the strip is nearly completed

Figure 25a. Hand shovelling a deluxe strip for a very cautious pilot

Figure 26. R.C.M.P. Twin Otter finally ready to take off Alexandra Fiord about 1979 or 1980

Rocky

Have you ever been down in the Arctic?

Not crashed, but just down and alone.

With blowing snow blanking your vision,

And the wind cutting through to the bone.

So, you lie curled up in a five star,

And hope your tent won't blow away.

While the snow whispers in through each opening,

And the night slowly eats at the day.

Then your mind slowly starts into wander,

And you think of the good times, all past.

Make a vow if you ever get southbound,

This trip to the north is your last.

But there's doubt in your mind that you'll make it.

Outside, it is forty below.

And the chances are slim, if there's any,

Of getting that aircraft to go.

So, you quickly return to your memories.

There are hundreds of good ones, I know.

There must be to keep you returning,

To this wasteland of ice and of snow.

The first years, it was for adventure.

You pushed it with all of your might,

With takeoffs in near zero-zero,

To fly through the black Arctic night.

At the end of the run was a party,

A bottle to share with your friends,

With never a thought for tomorrow,

"What the Hell? A hangover mends."

Then one day a quick look around you,

A bunch of your buddies are gone.

And the new ones just don't seem to make it,

They don't even sing the same song.

So, you claim that it's only the money

That brings you back, year after year.

You'll be out by the time you hit forty,

Still flying, but surely not here.

As the years slip on by, you will notice,

The parties and young girls fade fast.

Perhaps, in your mind, there's a glimmer,

That these fast, happy times just won't last.

Soon, one day, you'll find yourself talking,

About the good times, the days in the past,

And you'll realize nobody's listening.

They don't know anyone in the cast.

You'll put one more year in the Arctic,

One, two, or three, maybe four.

By then, you'll have enough money.

You won't have to work anymore.

But you know in your heart that you'll never

Save up quite enough to just quit,

And you're stuck flying here in the

Arctic, trip after trip after trip.

So, you lie in your bag and you wonder,

Just who in the hell's kidding who?

You're stuck in a rut, and you know it,

And there ain't a damn thing you can do.

When the wind stops blowing tomorrow,

And you're flying along in the sun,

You'll remember only the good times,

And know there's a bunch more to come.

So, keep up the pretense old timer.

It's all only part of the game.

If you're still flying here when you're sixty,

It's only yourself you can blame.

Astro Compass (Now Obsolete)

An Astro Compass is a great piece of equipment that has been used in polar navigation for years and will be for many more to come. (I made this statement before G.P.S. took over nearly all navigation.) This simple unit can tell you your aircraft heading with one simple sun, moon, or star shot. It was the main component of northern navigation prior to the advent of G.P.S. *The Air Almanac* gives a precise table of star, moon, and planet positions, and the only other required input is your longitudinal position which you should have a fairly close estimate of. Like all calculators and computers, the Astro Compass suffers from a malady known as G.I.=G.O. Garbage in, Garbage out.

The co-pilot assigned to me this evening was no stranger to the north. I had flown with him on two previous occasions with no problems, so I had no second thoughts when I asked him for a moon shot prior to beginning an approach at Grise Fiord, Canada's northernmost settlement. Grise Fiord is situated on a narrow shelf of rock that overlooks Jones sound. Steep cliffs rise to 4,500 feet directly behind the town and lower peaks of two to three thousand feet are prevalent on the two sides. One of the most picturesque spots in the Arctic, it is a tricky place for flying when weather conditions are less than perfect.

I anticipated no problems this evening as Grise weather was estimated at 1,500 feet overcast with six miles visibility in light snow. This was the last leg for the day, and I looked forward to the warm hospitality waiting for us at the R.C.M.P. house where we stayed.

My co-pilot held the astro compass so I could read the heading, and I dialed it into the gyroscope just as we crossed the beacon.

Turning outbound and reducing power, the aircraft dropped into the cloud with the moon's final light flickering across the instrument panel. Something was not right here; my eyes scanned the gauges, everything A.O.K. here but.... I added power and climbed back above the clouds. "Run that Astro Compass again will you; I can't quite believe the heading." I turned into the moon so he could get a good shot and again checked the figures against the aircraft gyroscope - right on. By this time, we were a good five miles from the beacon, and, as I turned back to start a new approach, I was still not convinced that things were right. I asked the co-pilot to explain the procedure for setting the Astro Compass. I listened in disbelief as he took the longitude for Grise Fiord, then subtracted the figure from the Almanac. "That's completely backward to what you should do," I said softly into the intercom. I turned back toward the moon and did a proper shot.

There was silence as I completed the approach and turned towards the faint lights of the village. "You don't need to get so mad, anyone can make a mistake."

"Yes," I thought, as I watched the dark cliff behind the town and off my right wing grow closer. Mistakes are easy to make, but in this business, you are often allowed none. In the future, I vowed to double-check all input.

Figure 27. An Astro Compass, used for celestial navigation before G.P.S. was available

Engine Failure

The Pratt and Whitney engines that power the Twin Otters are one of the most dependable engines ever built. In my twenty thousand plus hours, I had only two in-flight failures and four in flight shutdowns. This dependability let us operate in the most extreme weather conditions and in the most remote areas of the world. The peace of mind they provided made flights across the oceans of the world a non-event.

We were flying north along the coast of Baffin Island, having just completed a medivac from Pond Inlet to Frobisher Bay. The weather forecast for Pond was not that great, so we landed at Broughton Island (now known as Qikiqtarjuaq) for some extra fuel.

It was snowing lightly while we refuelled at Broughton Island and taxied out for the return trip to Pond Inlet. We topped the clouds at seven thousand feet and sat under a full moon at nine thousand feet. The cloud deck below was a bright grey with valleys of shadow that were ever changing as we flew north. Giving control to the co-pilot, I pushed back and closed my eyes. We had had a long day and Pond Inlet was still two hours away. Twenty minutes later, Brian woke me up to show me the left-hand fuel flow meter had climbed from the normal 270 pounds per hour up to the peg at six hundred pounds. Everything else looked normal, so we accepted it as a faulty gauge and continued north. About twenty minutes later, the right-hand fuel flow meter began to climb. This got our attention you can bet, and when the right engine shut down five minutes later, our lovely evening disappeared.

North of Clyde River, the mountains climb to five thousand feet plus and are separated by deep fiords, which were still open water. There was nowhere to land, and, with the cloud deck below us, a forced descent could mean only disaster. With only one engine turning, we had over an hour left to Pond Inlet. With the expectations of the other engine quitting at any moment, we had no choice but to continue north. The odds of getting to our destination were not good. "So, what are we going to do?" asked Brian.

"I don't know," I replied, "but for starters, go into the back and see if you can find some juice or pop or something, things are going to get very dry before this is over." We called the base in Resolute Bay and advised them of our predicament, but other than to be able to pass a few messages for family in the event of the worst, there was nothing to be done. After what was the longest one-hour period in my life, we started the approach at Pond Inlet. As would happen of course, Pond's weather had deteriorated, but there was no chance of making an alternate. So, the approach would end in a landing of one type or another.

I'll spare you the details of how bad the weather was, we've all heard too many of those stories. We did land on the runway and after shutdown, dropped the cowlings and pulled the fuel filters. The dead engine filter was a block of solid ice. The left filter had four of the filter corrugations open about one-eighth inch each. The rest was solid ice. It turned out that Broughton Island had received a new fuel truck on the sea lift that day, filled it with fuel, and delivered it to the airport. The old trucks all had filters on them, this truck did not. We drained approximately ten gallons of water out of the aircraft tanks. I have a great respect, which will never change, for the Pratt & Whitney engines.

The scary part of this story was the reaction of the Territorial Government when it was advised of the problem. Within a few days, they had rectified the problem, not by putting filters on the trucks, but by issuing a rubber stamp to all communities—stating that the fuel pumped was not certified for aircraft use.

The Black Polar Bear

In the back of my mind is a cavern,

A black, terror-filled sort of lair

That I keep boarded up, for inside it,

Lives what I call the Black Polar Bear.

For months, he will hibernate calmly.

You can almost forget he's around.

Then, something small will annoy him,

And snarling, he comes with a bound.

It may be an engine that shuts down,

Or a fire bell sounding in flight,

Or a simple fuel pressure flicker,

As you're flying along in the night.

Once out, he is often reluctant

To crawl back inside that small cave,

He'd rather be running 'round growling,

And making himself feel brave.

A checklist used faithfully certains

That he won't stick his nose out the door.

And a proper aircraft inspection,

Will help him continue to snore.

But, there's still uncontrollable factors

That you can't do a damn thing to fight,

Like a total electrical failure,

While you're straight I.F.R in the night.

Or sometimes when everything's perfect,

And you're cruising along in the clear,

He'll sneak up and quietly whisper,

A "what if, what's that" in your ear.

If you run through emergency systems,

Procedures, and how to respond,

By the time you are done, you will find that

The Black Polar Bear is long gone.

ALMOST

Arctic Gems

The Arctic spreads her emeralds below us, on display,

A hundred thousand tiny lakes, all glittering on this day.

With crystal rivers wandering across this barren land,

A modern artist's sketches traced by a giant hand.

Caribou and musk-ox herds are scattered here and there.

As with the gulls and Arctic terns,
we share the cool, clear air.

Flocks of swans dot the lakes below;
the young are turning white.

The snow geese stage along the coast
before their southern flight.

The evening shadows lengthen now,
forewarning all at hand,

That very soon there will be no light,
and snow will rule the land.

But, for today, enjoy your flight, yes, take in all you view.

Perhaps, throughout the winter night,
this will all come back to you.

We Honestly Didn't Know

Matt and I had a day trip to Quanak in Greenland and had a few hours to wander around town. We bought a couple carvings and took some pictures of the Greenlanders and their houses. Scouting through the local store, we found some Danish chocolate bars and, lo and behold, cases of Heineken beer. "Beer? Beer! Wow!" We pooled our remaining money and managed to buy eight cases of twenty-four cans each.

When we got back to Resolute, the party was on. We split the cost with everyone who came, and things were going great—pizza and cold beer, and no shortage of friends that night. About 10:30 p.m., just when things were rolling, someone, I don't know who, hollered, "Whoa!" and read the label on the can. "Non-Alcoholic Beer? What!!" Honestly, we didn't know 'till just then, and, though a couple air radio clowns wanted their money back, the rest of the group decided it was too good a party to shut down for a minor detail like that.

The River

I was on my way back to Resolute after a trip to Northern Greenland, putting out a couple caches of fuel barrels. Resolute called and asked if I could stop in at Lake Hazen to do an inventory of the supplies that were left prior to the beginning of our spring tourist season, and I readily agreed to do it. I loved the camp at Hazen and was more than happy to land there and spend the night.

After walking up to the camp from the lake, I fired up a Preway heater, then started the Ski-Doo, loaded a few water jugs, and headed down to the river for some water. Where the river flowed over a shallow gravel ridge out of the lake, it remained open throughout the winter, even in the minus forty-degree temperatures.

Parking the Ski-Doo a safe distance from the ice edge, I took two water jugs and headed for the river. Twenty feet from the edge, the ice broke, plunging me into about six feet of very cold and swiftly flowing water. Getting myself out was no easy feat with quilted coveralls, winter boots, and a down-filled parka that absorbed water like a sponge. I did get out and, luckily for me, the Ski-Doo started with the first pull. Water jugs forgotten, I headed back to the camp. By the time I got there, my clothing had frozen solid, and I had trouble moving off the Ski-Doo. When I got to the door of the Parkall, I couldn't open it and, instead, leaned into it until the latch broke. Thankfully, the oil heater that I had started was going full bore, and I was soon stripped off and wrapped in a blanket. I melted snow for my water needs and never went to the river again when I was alone. I was lucky to survive that incident.

Mike

Mike was planning a walking trip to the North Pole the following year, and he had contacted us to do the flying support that he would require. We offered him a job helping out at our base camp at Lake Hazen on Ellesmere Island, our jumping off point for tourist trips to the North Pole. Flying with us, while putting out fuel caches, would give him an opportunity to see what he would be up against while on the ocean ice, and we could always use help around the camp.

Leaving Mike at the camp while I flew a load of tourists back to Resolute where I would pick up another group the next day, I cautioned him to stay away from the river that flowed out of the lake as on more than one occasion someone had broken through the ice. This was about the only trouble he could get into, or so I thought.

Well, as it turned out, the flight from the south could not land due to weather, and our incoming tourist's arrival in Resolute was delayed for three to four days. In the meantime, I was called over to Rae Point, the base camp of Panarctic Oils, to do some support work for their rigs. Busy using the Rae Point radio frequency, I was unaware of the conversations between Lake Hazen and CJM-76, our Resolute base radio, until a radio operator at one of the rigs joined me for breakfast. "That's quite a problem you have at Hazen." he offered.

"Huh, what's that?" I said.

"Well, sounds like the wolves have attacked the guy up there, and he is holed up in the camp. He has been calling for the

Fish and Wildlife guy to fly up and save him. It's the laugh of the Arctic just now."

"Oh man, what next?" I went to the aircraft and called Res base to find out that, indeed, they were being called several times a day by Mike about the wolves.

Now the wolves in the Arctic and especially those in remote areas like Hazen are not dangerous. In fact, I had often had them sniffing around my feet while refuelling. They would steal fish off the porch of the camp and sit eating them a few short yards away. While they had no fear of humans, they also were no threat and, in fact, were quite playful. Talking to Mike on the radio, he insisted that they had chased him back to the camp, and he was scared. Well, we were not about to do a flight for this, so it was another two days before I headed north with our new tourists. In the meantime, every rig I landed at had new stories and much laughter about the situation.

Finally, landing on the lake, I asked the passengers to wait at the airplane while I went up to the camp to talk to Mike. I was about halfway up the hill to the camp when the door burst open, and Mike came running out, waving his arms and shouting, "Go back, go back, they're still here, they're still here!" Then, he turned and ran back into the Parkall and slammed the door. I continued up the hill and, yes, there were some signs of wolves around the place, but no more than usual and certainly nothing to cause alarm.

I tried to explain to him that the wolves would come to investigate any movement but certainly would not attack. It was impossible to convince him that his life had not been in jeopardy, so I put him on the resupply aircraft that arrived later that day and sent him back to Resolute Bay. I had to take him to the aircraft on a Ski-Doo because he was still too afraid to walk down the hill.

I've Got a Truck Like That

The military background of the man hired as chief pilot just didn't fit in with a bush pilot crew who were experienced, self reliant, and with flying abilities that could never be obtained in the military. There was a total lack of respect on both sides; they would never come to terms. This story will not dwell on this theme, though it certainly played a part in what was to happen.

The chief pilot had decided that we would do our crew change out of Inuvik with one of the company aircraft. Not a bad idea as we had four to five crew headed south. I was in filing the flight plan to Edmonton with a fuel stop at Fort Simpson when the Chief Pilot came up beside me and said, "Put my name in as the captain as I am the senior pilot on board."

"Well," I replied, "if that's the case, not only can you fly the trip, but you can file the flight plan." I had been flying all day and really was looking forward to sitting in the back of a 737 with a book and a Scotch, not flying a Twin Otter south.

An hour later, we were airborne, and the four of us in the back had a card game going with a few drinks to go with it. While refuelling at Fort Simpson, we were given a lecture about the fun we were having in the back and also advised that we would be stopping in Dawson Creek for three to four hours, while he met with the owner of the company. This was unacceptable to all of us for various reasons, for example, my wife was driving over a hundred miles to pick me up, and I had given her an ETA so she could meet me.

Brian and I decided we would not go along with this, and we pulled our bags out of the aircraft and watched as the lights disappeared in the southern sky. We phoned our friend, Ted Grant, who owned Simpson Air and asked if he could pick us up and put us up for the night. "Sure", he said "but you will have to sleep in the tent as we have company in the house."

The next morning, Brian and I were walking toward the town strip, trying to figure out how we were going to get home, when a truck with four Indians in it went rattling by. "Hey, I've got a truck like that leased to Ted; it's in a lot better shape, and Ted promised not to let the Indians use it. The lease is up, and we could take it to Fort Smith if we can't get a plane from here." We couldn't find anyone with a flight headed south, and we were in Ted's office when this same truck pulled in.

"Here's your truck now," Ted said.

With a dozen cold beers and a couple hamburgers, we headed out for Fort Smith. Driving that truck down the gravel was something akin to herding a goat, but after a flat tire, no spare, and a tire borrowed from the next truck coming down the road, it handled much better. Brian dropped me at the Fort Smith airport just in time to get the jump seat on a Pacific Western flight to Edmonton. I arrived a day later than I would have if I'd stayed with the company aircraft—but what the hell?

Ugi Lake

Brian Robertson had a contract to position fuel barrels on a lake south of Baker Lake and called for me to crew the Twin Otter for support. In those days, we flew the Twin Otters single pilot and, due to the small amount of flying involved, I did not have an engineer with me either.

We left Yellowknife about 6:00 a.m. and flew to Baker Lake for fuel, then down to Ugi Lake to prepare a strip for P.W.A.'s Herc, which would come later in the afternoon with a Parkall tent and a small Cat. When we landed, it was below -40° and stayed that way all day as the crew of six, plus me, hand shovelled the major drifts out of the planned landing area. The Herc arrived, dropped our camp and the Cat, then had an engine failure due to snow ingestion on takeoff. We could see a lot of hand action in the cockpit as it struggled into the air.

We got the Parkall set up and covered, but just did the basics for tie-down because it was late and cold. With the oil stove running full blast, we dug out sleeping bags and our personal gear from the Twin Otter and chewed some frozen sandwiches. A drink was in order, but all the bottles were frozen to the point that we could not get a pour—Ballantine's Scotch, frozen; Canadian Club, frozen; Smirnoff Vodka, frozen. One bottle was pourable—Bacardi pink cap over-proof rum. We had set some Coke on the heater, and it was actually warm by this time. However, adding it to the rum in a Styrofoam cup created a slushy you could eat with a spoon. Well, a few of those and everyone was sound asleep. When the wind came up four hours later, we were all taking laces out of our boots and scrambling to tie the Parkall covers together to keep things from self-destructing. It was a horrible night, and we were all so tired from a tough, cold day, we could certainly have done without that.

Icebergs

Figure 28. An iceberg of this size would probably have come off a glacier in Greenland

If you have spent some time along the east coast of the Arctic, you have probably noticed that the number of icebergs sailing down Baffin Bay has decreased drastically over the past forty years or so. This is a direct result of the use of engine-driven ships. Years ago, when sail power was the main method of propulsion, an iceberg would break away from the glacier and immediately head out of the fiord to begin plotting an attack on the nearest sailing ship.

Records show that devious methods were utilized. It was not uncommon for an iceberg to skulk about in a fog bank, sneaking up on an unwary schooner, then leaping out of the clag with nary a sound of warning, to cause damage or death.

Many ships were killed or badly injured in these encounters. The advent of diesel- and steam-powered ships was declared foul play by the icebergs who now tended to sulk and refuse to leave the fiords. Watching their predecessors plan and launch attack after attack only to have the ship dodge to one side or the other while the iceberg sailed by, often becoming impaled on a reef or slamming into the shore ice to die hopelessly trapped, seemed to remove all desire from the young bergs to head for the open sea. Radar development was just another reason to lie around the old fiord.

In 1979, an all-out attack was launched against the Arctic Star, a small, wooden ship that was working the east Baffin area when her engines quit. Icebergs from as far away as northern Greenland sailed forth to lay claim to their crippled prize. As luck would have it, the ship lay nestled behind a shoal north of Clyde River. At least twenty icebergs piled up on the reef to die a slow death, being eaten by waves and the summer sun.

With the establishment of fixed-position drilling platforms, some of the larger icebergs left the fiords and began a long voyage to southern waters in a valiant attempt to collide with one of these seemingly vulnerable platforms. The years of sitting in the fiords seem to have taken their toll, however, as these young bergs just don't seem to have the long-range planning ability of their ancestors; they often sail by, no closer than ten or twenty miles to the target.

It seems the traditional heritage that was handed down from the bergs of years gone by has been forgotten by these younger bergs, which now seem unable to take advantage of even a stationary object. This is the reason you will find more and more icebergs hanging out in the fiords with little or no inclination to head out to the open sea. There are still a few diehards that, with the memory of the Titanic instilled in their minds, will press forward in a valiant attempt to ram some unsuspecting ship. Perhaps, some new success will bring forth a concentrated effort. For the time being, however, things look bleak indeed for future generations of icebergs.

Polar Bear Attack

I was flying out of Frobisher Bay, now called Iqaluit, when a call came in for a medivac flight from a small Inuit community called Kimmirut, about sixty-five miles to the west. While we were loading the patient onto the aircraft, he kept saying, "I'm blind, I'm blind." When we landed at Iqaluit, the nurse who came with the ambulance climbed in and did a quick assessment of the patient. While doing so, the nurse pushed the man's torn scalp up from his face. "I can see, I can see." he cried. He had been terrified about being blind and was so relieved to find he was not.

The story I got from one of the guides went like this. They were guiding some American hunters on a caribou hunt and had made their camp on a ridge just above where they had parked the boat they were using. The guide insisted that the hunters unload their guns prior to taking them into the tent.

At some point in the early morning hours, a polar bear came into camp and proceeded to tear into the guide's tent. Kooto, one of the native guides, ran out of the tent and tripped over one of the tie-down ropes. The bear jumped on him, tearing at his back and head, then grabbed him by the ankle and started dragging him away. The hunters were scrambling around trying to find bullets and guns without much success. The second guide finally got out of the tent and shot the bear, but a lot of damage had been done by then. Loading Kooto into the canoe, they headed into Kimmirut and called for the airplane.

I visited Kooto a year or so after this attack, and he showed me some of the damage the bear had done to him. His back is badly scarred, and he has quite a scar where the bear nearly tore his scalp off.

Figure 29. Kooto and I—a few years after the attack

My First Trip to the Geographic North Pole, May 2, 1978

On April 30th, Japanese adventurer, Naomi Uemura completed his solo dog team trip from Cape Columbia, Canada's northernmost land point, to the Geographic North Pole. His journey started on March 6th and was the first solo trip to the Pole. On May 2nd, I left Resolute Bay to pick him off the ice. This was my first of what was to turn into many trips to this top of the world.

In those days, we flew the Twin Otters as single pilot aircraft and, because of the long duration of the flight and the numerous fuel barrels that would be needed, I asked Tom Frook, our base manager, for a helper. "There is just no one around," he said, and then offered me our cook's helper, Lois Ennis. It took a bit of convincing to get her to come with me as she was not really into flying. She finally consented, and we departed Resolute about 11:00 a.m. with three Japanese passengers, three frozen seals, and two drums of fuel.

After a fuel stop at Grise Fiord, we flew to Alert, a military base on the north end of Ellesmere Island, where we dropped the passengers, seals, and fuel drums. From there, we backtracked to our camp at Lake Hazen, refuelled the aircraft, loaded six barrels of fuel, and departed for the Pole. Landing at Pole at 10:00 p.m., we didn't even think of the fact that this made Lois the second woman to ever be at the North Pole, the first being Weldy Phipps's wife, Fran.

We refuelled; loaded Naomi, fifteen dogs, the sleigh, miscellaneous gear, and two photographers; and began a takeoff roll that had to be aborted. The second attempt was successful, though very rough, and we were on our way back to Alert.

Lois was not very impressed with the takeoff, and it was an hour or so before she relaxed. She tensed up again at Alert because the weather had closed in, and we made two attempts at landing before we were able to get down.

After unloading the dogs, passengers, and equipment, we pumped in the two barrels of fuel that we had cached at Alert and departed for Lake Hazen to refuel. After a fuel stop at Grise Fiord, we arrived at Resolute Bay about 11:00 a.m. Twenty-four hours with two sandwiches and a few cans of juice, it was time for a steak, eggs, and some sleep.

Figure 30. Lois, Naomi and Harry at North Pole May 3rd, 1978

Ridiculous Ideas

After we started doing some tourist trips to the geographic North Pole in 1978, we started getting some of the craziest requests. For example, a woman phoned from somewhere in Florida, asking if we could take her and her pink Cadillac to the Pole on New Year's Eve, so she could drive around the world with the top down. Another guy showed up with a bicycle with chocolate bars stuffed in the handlebars, convinced he could ride it to the Pole. A renowned Japanese sailor arrived, unannounced, with an ice boat and a support crew, convinced that he could sail to the Pole as if it were Lake Simcoe. Trying to explain the impassable ice conditions he would encounter proved to be impossible, and it wasn't until we descended over the coastline and he saw the huge pressure ridges that reality started to set in.

Figure 31. This iceboat actually broke on a trial trip across the bay at Resolute, which is basically smooth. My friend Stan, standing by the boat, is of Polish descent, and we decided that was as close to a Pole as it would ever get.

Potato Chips

Tom Frook was the base manager in Resolute Bay when I first arrived there in 1977. He was a great guy with lots of fun ideas. Let's get the work done and have some fun seemed his motto. We are both out of the industry now but remain best of friends though we live 3,500 miles apart.

Tom and I were sitting in a corner of the hangar with a bottle of Scotch, looking at a small mountain of nylon postal bags. Government subsidized food mail was an important part of our business, yet somehow it didn't seem right to have two airplane loads of potato chips arrive the day after we did two loads of meat and canned goods. Had everything arrived together, we could have moved everything in two trips, now we were faced with two extra trips to move these bulky chips that we felt should not even be included on the eligible list for subsidized food mail.

As the level of Scotch in the bottle went down, the pile of mail bags seemed to grow, and the talk turned to reducing the bulk of this pile. Well, a few more drinks and the answer became crystal clear. The little Caterpillar tow unit we had was equipped with rubber pads and was parked in a corner of the hanger. Whisky prevailed over wisdom, and the huge pile of potato chip bags was soon reduced to half an Otter load. We never did hear anything back about this little stunt, but we did notice that there were no shipments of potato chips to that community for some time.

While we are talking about potato chips—years later, the suppliers were packaging chips in small plastic bags that were pressurized with some type of gas to extend shelf life, I guess.

Then they were packed into cardboard boxes. The minimum altitude across the mountains from Pangnirtung to Broughton Island, now called Qikiqtarjuaq, was 9,100 feet and that was about two thousand feet more than these little bags could take. You could hear them exploding like popcorn in the back of the aircraft.

Mould Bay Incident 1990

It was the final day of a nice contract installing sonar buoys under the Arctic ice. Working out of Mould Bay, a remote weather station in the high Canadian Arctic, we were on the way back from our most distant location. Almost north of Russia, the logistics had required a fuel cache for use both out and back.

The day had gone well, and we refuelled and loaded the empty drums just before sunset. Levelling off at eight thousand feet, I punched on the autopilot, poured a cup of lukewarm coffee from the thermos, and settled in for the three-hour flight back to Mould Bay. Weather from there was not great but nothing we couldn't handle, and there was nowhere else to go anyway. Prior to descent, I called for and received the weather: -31°C visibility one-quarter mile in blowing snow with winds out of the north at twenty-seven knots. The ceiling was estimated at one thousand feet. Turning off the autopilot for the descent, I trimmed ahead on the wheel, only to have the aircraft respond with a slight raising of the nose. Pushing forward on the controls, I found that the elevator would not move. Applying both forward and back pressure on the controls proved useless, and the realization of a major problem hit home.

Under the right conditions, an aircraft can be flown to a landing without much use of elevators. Reducing power will cause descent and applying power will cause a climb. All well and good in calm air and with lots of landing area. We were missing a lot of ingredients to make this landing work. The winds were about ninety degrees to the strip and, as they came across the ridge, the mechanical turbulence created would cause major problems.

The runway crew advised that they were having problems keeping the flare pots lit, and suggested they park their pickup at the near end of the strip. This would not work, as with the lack of control, I needed them away from the landing area. Descending through two thousand feet and about six miles back on a long final, we started getting into the rough air. The aircraft nosed down and, at one point, we were seven hundred feet and descending at over one thousand feet per minute. Full power and full forward trim ever so slowly corrected the descent then started a climb. Power off and the nose dropped. We plowed into the runway nose wheel first, then bounced back into the night to hit again about two hundred feet further down the runway in a flat attitude and hard enough to break the skis, skidding to a stop crossways to the runway with the broken nose wheel just starting down the steep edge. The last radio talk I heard was the truck saying we had landed in front of them and then taken off again.

I got out the front door and let the two passengers out the back. We couldn't see more than a few feet in the darkness and blowing snow, but I asked them to walk down the runway until they found the parking area where the truck was. No one was seriously injured, and subsequent investigation showed that an accumulation of ice, caused by snow that melted in the cabin, had filled a small compartment that the control cables ran through. The melted snow had frozen around the cables and a small turnbuckle and seized the controls. We were alive and happy to be. A very lucky outcome to a very scary time. The Twin Otter is a tough old airplane—as it proved that night.

Figure 32. This little bit of ice caused all the problem.

Figure 33. Damage caused by landing with no elevator control.

Transportation Safety Board of Canada | Bureau de la sécurité des transports du Canada

Western Region - Air
Suite 12, 14220 Yellowhead Trail
Edmonton, Alberta
T5L 3C2

Our file Notre référence
90W0071

25 January 1991

Mr. Harry Hanlan
P.O. Box 2159,
Canmore, AB.
T0L 0M0

Dear Mr. Hanlan:

Enclosed you will find a copy of a letter from de Havilland in response to our conditional draft report involving C-FSJB at Mould Bay, Northwest Territories.

I wanted you to be aware of their comments in general and, more specifically, their tribute to your success in that landing. We certainly agree with that assessment.

Hope you are having a good winter and many more successful landings.

Yours truly,

L. E. Ulrich
Operations Investigator
TSB - Air
Western Region

Canada

Figure 34. Letter from the Transport Safety Board of Canada

Boeing of Canada Ltd.
de Havilland Division
Garratt Boulevard
Downsview, Ontario,
Canada M3K 1Y5

Telephone 416-633-7310

September 27, 1990
D.3860.JD.242

John W. Stants
C.T.A.I.S.B.
P.O. Box 9120
Alta Vista Terminal
OTTAWA, Ontario
K1G 3T8

Dear Sir:

SUBJECT: DRAFT AVIATION OCCURRENCE REPORT 90W0071 (0259)
MOULD BAY, NORTHWEST TERRITORIES, MARCH 23, 1990

We appreciate the opportunity to comment on the above
referenced report. We concur with this report and offer the
following comments.

For the case of a jammed elevator control circuit, as was
experienced in this accident, the effect of elevator trim tab
application will indeed have minimal effect on longitudinal
control.

The need to land C-FSJB in a 27 knot 100 degree crosswind
made this particular landing task extremely difficult. The
success is a tribute to the pilot.

In closing, it is our opinion that although substantial
quantities of snow were introduced to the aircraft cabin pre-
liftoff, it is believed that the buildup observed during post
occurrence inspection had accumulated over a longer period of
time. We believe that during continued operation in
environments similar to that of C-FSJB, it is possible for an
ice buildup to occur following moisture introduction by
passengers, on cargo or through a poorly sealed inspection
panel and this moisture not drain properly due to the
aircraft's continued exposure to sub-zero temperatures.

As a result, we are in the process of introducing an
inspection procedure into the DHC-6 Inspection Requirements
Manual and a "CAUTION" into the All Weather Operation Section
of the DHC-6 Supplementary Operating Data Manual to reduce
the possibility of future occurrences of this nature.

Yours truly,

Jim Donnelly,
Product Safety Manager

JD:bsd

Figure 35. Letter from Boeing of Canada

First Ferry Flight to Burma (Ferry Trip from Hell)

In 1990, Kenn Borek Air had received a contract from Canadian Helicopters to supply a Twin Otter for some work in Burma. The contract called for the aircraft to arrive within a limited time, and so a hectic preparation and ferry flight began.

Taxiing back to the hanger for the third time, it was beginning to look like we would have to delay our departure for a day. I had returned from the run-up area again because one of the engines would not produce full power, yet when the engineers ran it up, all was fine. Finally, I took the engineers with me, and we figured out that they were doing run-ups with the bleed air valves in the off position. I was doing run-ups with them in the normal, on position. This diagnosis indicated a bleed air valve failure, and when a new valve was installed all was good to go. There are two of these valves and with a normal flight it was not a no-go item. This flight was going to be far from normal with a long leg across the Pacific, requiring the in-flight refuelling that the air valves were used for. We got a late start but made it to Whitehorse in time to get a pizza for a late meal. In the morning, I taxied out, leaving Margo, my wife, waving to me from the tarmac. She was meeting a friend from Antarctica for a few days before returning to Calgary.

We spent the next afternoon in Anchorage, arranging for fuel and accommodation at the American base on Adak Island, one of the westernmost islands in the Aleutian Island chain. I think because we had flown with the United States Navy in Antarctica earlier in the year, we were given the OK to fuel and overnight there.

Later that night, I was questioning why we were there. We were taken by military escort to a fast-food restaurant, then to our room in a wooden barracks where we were locked into our rooms. It was a Friday night and, as we listened to the other occupants returning to their rooms in all states of drunken revelry, the thought of our helplessness in case of a fire caused us a restless night. The next morning, we fuelled the aircraft's main tanks, wingtip tanks, two large internal tanks, six 45- gallon drums, and twelve 5-gallon jugs. Add the aircraft spares, engineer's tools, personal baggage, and miscellaneous stuff, we were fairly heavy. Adak control asked us to climb to eight thousand feet, which we were unable to reach until about three hours later, after some fuel burn off.

Working our way across the Pacific headed for Japan, we reported to Hawaii Air Traffic Control every hour with an approximate position. G.P.S. wasn't in place yet. Reporting as we neared Japan, the Hawaii controller replied, "My God, you boys still in the air? I was working you last night before I went home." Pretty funny.

About that time, Japan called to tell us to turn around and return because we did not have the necessary clearance permission to land there. Well, that was impossible, so we continued on, wondering why the paperwork was not in place. Entirely my fault; I should never have left without having it physically in hand. Upon landing, fourteen hours and seventeen minutes after takeoff, we were surrounded by jeeps, machine guns, and a fuel truck and advised we would be refuelled, then we had to return to Adak. After many hours in an office where I tried to explain that it must be a paper error and that there was no way I was going to fly the aircraft back across the Pacific, it was agreed that we would be placed under house arrest at a hotel until we could sort things out. When the security chief asked to see the ongoing paperwork for Taiwan and Thailand, my paper excuse was ruined. With the help of the Canadian Embassy, we were allowed to leave the hotel from 8:00 a.m. to 8:00 p.m. daily, which helped a lot.

In all, we were tied up for four days before I could obtain the necessary overflight permits and landing clearances. During that time, there was a major typhoon in the area of Kagoshima, one of our planned fuel stops, which would have prevented us from continuing anyway. So, the contract was not in jeopardy.

Finally, we had enough paperwork in hand to depart and after an overnight stop in Kagoshima, we headed for Taipei in Taiwan where we overnighted without incident. The next day, it was late afternoon when we landed in Da Nang, Vietnam, where we were advised that Laos would not allow us to fly over their country. We would be forced to detour quite a way south to go around. What should have been a fuel stop turned into an overnight stay, and after much haggling behind a closed office door, we got authorization to stay over. A closed door always indicated trouble that only cash money could solve, and this was no exception. I am sure that the taxi and hotel we were taken to were owned by relatives of the security officer, and we were ripped off very badly.

Departing the next morning, we were in Bangkok by late afternoon, where we were met by Thai Airlines ground personnel and assured that all was well. They showed us where to park, then took us right through customs and immigration and to our hotel. The best arrival of the whole trip. One more leg of about three hours and we arrived in Rangoon. The ferry trip from hell was finally finished.

Burma (Now Myanmar) 1990

The company I worked for, Kenn Borek Air, had been approached by Canadian Helicopters to supply a Twin Otter as part of a contract they were bidding to support four oil companies in Burma. When the contract was awarded, Canadian Helicopters did not get the chopper part of the contract but did get the Twin Otter part. Subsequently, I ended up in Rangoon with an Otter and a crew of three.

The Canadian Helicopter representative met us in Bangkok on his way home to Canada. He gave us the address of the house he had rented for us, the name of the cook, and the name of a local expediter who was to look after our needs. The cook was good, the expediter less than. The rental cars we had on arrival were taken away shortly after we arrived for nonpayment of the account. There were no car rental companies as such, and the cars were from friends of the expediter. The oil companies wanted us flying ASAP, but we could do nothing until the plane was blessed by the monks. This took a few days to get done. The military government insisted that we carry one of their navigators on board at all times. I really don't think he had a clue where we were most of the time, but he did make sure we didn't wander away from the airplane at the small airports we landed at. They didn't want us talking to anyone, and the people would not talk to us in fear of a late-night visit from the authorities. Everywhere we went in Rangoon, we were followed by three to four government men.

You must understand that just a year before, the military had shot down students who were protesting in the streets. One day, my co-pilot, against all our advice, was seen taking pictures from the window of our car. Within a few blocks, we were pulled into a side street and sat for half an hour with machine guns pointed in the windows while our driver was taken for questioning. I'm not sure how he talked our way out of that, but he was some scared when we finally got underway.

The Japanese oil company that was kind of in charge of the aircraft use basically ignored us in all aspects but the flying. It wasn't until my wife, Margo, arrived and started meeting with the American wives that we began to be included in the social life. The Americans took us under their wing and invited to us join the American Embassy Club with all its facilities and included us in their parties, outings, and so forth. Life improved greatly from then on.

Being a service company to oil companies meant we were the poor folk on the block, and the difference was staggering. The house that four of us shared had no air-conditioning and no power backup to cope with the scheduled and unscheduled power outages. Minimum furniture, and the maid washed our clothes on a cement block in the back yard. Clothes didn't last long with that treatment. One saving grace was when one of the oil company families went out of country for a week or so, they would offer us their air-conditioned house while they were gone. We hated to see them come back.

Once we were in the mainstream of the social life, it was a great place to be. We had loads of fun and made some great friends. Tennis, softball, swimming, hash house runs, and parties nearly every weekend made some great memories.

Keep It Simple

Flying in third world countries involves a lot of confusion when information is passed over radios to operators who, at best, have a limited understanding of English. They can generally get by if the wording is what they expect to hear or if simple wording is used. The words yes, no, affirmative and negative, roger and wilco are pretty well universally accepted. An acronym that is often used to remind new crewmen to emphasize the necessity of simple language is KISS (keeps it simple, stupid).

Sometimes it takes a while for the concept to sink in. Take this example of a conversation between a Canadian Helicopter pilot and a Burmese radio operator, who had it all together, up to a point.

"Yangon, this is Helo c-fxxx inbound from the rig with a medivac, requesting clearance."

"c-fxxx Yangon, cleared to the airport for an approach, call final. ...do you require an ambulance?"

Well now, a simple no or negative would have worked, no problem. But the answer came back, "The patient is ambulatory." The ambulance was waiting when the helicopter arrived. ... surprise, surprise.

Vanuatu

Located about twelve hundred miles north and east of Australia and once called the New Hebrides Islands, Vanuatu consists of a chain of eighty-three islands of various sizes. I was on my way home from Antarctica in December, 1995 when I got a call from some friends I had met in Burma a few years earlier. They were now flying in Vanuatu and invited me to come for a visit. I would be landing in Christchurch and was due for some time off, so I accepted. It was a wonderful place, and I fell in love with the short jungle strips and the happy, fun-loving people. I asked Vanair, the local carrier, if they would be able to use me if I came back the next year, and they were happy to offer me a position. I returned for two months in 1996 and again in 1997 on my way home from Antarctica. It was fun flying and a perfect change after three months on the ice.

Figure 36. The terminal on one of the smaller islands

Figure 37. A typical island airstrip

Pig tusks were still used as currency on some of the islands, and there were often two or three pigs included in the baggage. They were stuffed into either a gunny or plastic sack that had a hole cut in one corner, so their snout could stick out to breath. It seemed impossible for a local to walk by one of these poor pigs lying on the tarmac without giving it a kick to make it squeal. They were loaded in with the bags—if they were lucky, they might be on top; if not, then the bottom. It didn't matter much to the loaders.

Figure 38. Pigs waiting for their flight.

Chickens were another valued item that were transported regularly. They were treated much better than the pigs and were usually carried on board. Two roosters in their own little container woven out of palm leaf, attached to a small stick were hand carried.

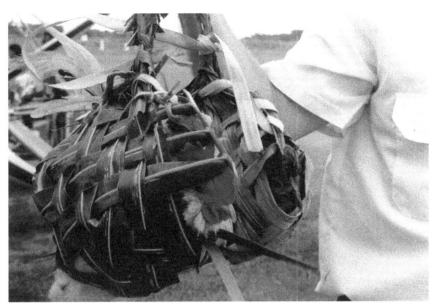

Figure 39. Roosters travelled first class.

There were lots of children, and the regulations allowed children under, I think, eight-years-old to sit three to a two-seat row. Adults could also hold a child under three on their laps. It took a while to get used to showing a passenger load of over thirty on a twenty-seat aircraft.

Home of bungee jumping, a ritual originally thought to insure a successful yam crop, Pentecost Islanders still use the jumping ritual as a rite of passage into manhood. Weaving their own vines and calculating the length to just brush the ground, they leap from a tower of up to 60 feet in height.

Figure 39a. Ritual dancing on the Island of Tanna

Figure 39b. A group of young men watch the dancing

Bushman

The airstrips on the remote islands of Vanuatu were mostly grass, carved out of the jungle that encroached on the perimeter of the strip and taxiway.

As I was about to leave, the agent told me that he was waiting for one passenger who was headed for the hospital on Santos, one of the major islands. Minutes later, a small man, a native bushman, well under five feet, with a quiver of arrows on his back and a bow almost as long as he was tall, in his hand, stepped out of the jungle and headed toward the aircraft. Dressed in only a banana leaf penis sheath, it was not a thing of beauty watching him climb the ladder into the airplane. I thought how brave he must be to step out of his world and get into a tin bird for the first time. He sat stock still, staring straight ahead as I buckled his seat belt. I think perhaps he had smoked or chewed something prior to coming to the plane because his demeanour never changed during takeoff or during the flight. The only concession to progress seemed to be attached to his bow, a small leather pouch holding a spray can of OFF.

Kyrgyzstan

In 1996, I was flying for a Canadian mining company in Kyrgyzstan when a Russian Helicopter crew invited us to a party at a dacha in the surrounding hills. I accepted on behalf of my crew, and, on the party night, our driver took us to the summer house of the chief of police of Bishkek. A party of about forty people was just getting started as we arrived at the gate. Hanging over the gate were two fresh sheep skins, and we gathered that we would be having sheep for dinner.

Walking through the kitchen area, we saw about six women preparing and cooking. Large tubs set in concrete over wood fires contained boiling water or had hot oil bubbling in them. Platters of appetizers soon started to appear. It took awhile for us to figure out what they were, little deep-fried bows and strips of meat. Tasted great, but it was a little hard to get past the idea that we were eating the intestines and strips of stomach. Later would come liver and heart, then the meat itself—served on a long table at which many guests were seated. A toast was proposed every few minutes, and your shot glass was to be drained every time. Only the person making the toast was exempt from this custom, and we were not really able to take that position. Well, as the evening progressed more and more of our Russian hosts were assisted from the table and taken home. My crew held up very well, and the folklore of hard-drinking Russians seemed questionable.

Back to the meal. When the main course started to appear, a platter with a whole sheep head was brought in, and while I hoped it would go to the other end of the table, that was not to be. I was the guest of honour, and the head was bestowed on me. When I say I didn't have a clue what I was going to do, you better believe it. As everyone sat there waiting for me to do something, my mind was going a mile a minute in a bit of a vodka fog. I cut one of the ears off and passed it to the person on my left. That seemed OK. So, I carved off the other ear and passed it to the right. Then I had what proved to be a brainstorm; I picked up the platter and knife, then walked to the senior helicopter pilot and asked if he would please do me the honour of serving this. Everyone clapped, another toast was proposed, and the meal continued.

A bit later in the evening, the chief of police and I were talking. He asked if we were having any problems in town. I explained that we were often stopped by armed personnel and asked for cigarettes and, in some cases, money was more demanded than asked for. This was especially true for my engineer who was of small stature. Almost every time we came home late, we were accosted and delayed if we did not donate something. Our papers would be examined, and we would be questioned for long periods. The police chief reached into his pocket, brought out three business cards, and wrote a phone number on each of them. "Keep these with you. The next time you get stopped, first take out your cell phone, and then show this card and start dialing the number. You will probably be alone by then, but if not, pass the phone to them and your problems will be over." Well, we never ever got past showing the card, and very soon we were only nodded at and wished a good evening.

First Antarctic Contract

In 1984, the National Science Foundation approached Kenn Borek Air to ask if we could offer a contract to supply a Twin Otter on skis to work with their scientists in Antarctica. I was given the opportunity to take on this project and accepted it immediately. N.S.F. sent three representatives to our hangar in Calgary to look over our aircraft and show us the special equipment that would have to be put onto and into the aircraft. The engineers at Borek did a fabulous job of putting this all together in record time. In the meantime, Steve Penikett the company manager, Glenna Kells the office manager, and I went to meetings in Washington to get a better understanding of what was expected of our operation.

Listening to the Hercules pilots who operated the ski-equipped Hercs expound over and over about how harsh the flying conditions were and how we would be lucky to accomplish anything "down there" got really old in a hurry. Our planned crew of three— myself, Bob Allen as second Captain, and Dave Baker the engineer had many years of Arctic experience, which would prove to be totally adequate for the job. In fact, we were able to operate with few problems and had very few no-fly days. This was the start of many contracts for our aircraft and crews, and, in 2015, I think there were close to fifteen of Borek's airplanes operating for various countries, including the United States, in Antarctica.

This was our first ferry flight to Antarctica and was a big learning trip that took a lot of time other than the actual flying. Where the different offices for customs and immigration were located, where to get fuel, will they accept our credit cards, where can you find a taxi? Different currencies and exchange rates. Where can we exchange money for local purchases, that is, for meals, taxis, and so forth? Some places would take U.S. dollars at terrible rates, some wouldn't accept anything but the local money. All this information helped speed up future trips, but for this one it proved very time-consuming.

Our routing and dates follow:

- November 1 Depart Calgary for Kansas City, 6.4 hours, overnight

- November 2 to Miami, 7.3 hours, fuel stop then to Barranquilla, Columbia, 6.4 hours, overnight

- November 3 to Guayaquil, Ecuador, 6.0 hours, overnight

- November 4 to Lima, Peru, 4.7 hours, fuel stop then to Antofagasta, Chile, 5.0 hours, overnight

- November 5 to Puerto Montt, Chile, 6.2 hours, overnight

- November 6 to Punta Arenas, Chile, 4.7 hours, 2 nights

- November 7 unload and put on the skis

- November 8 to Rothera, Antarctica, 7.6 hours

- We were held in Rothera until November 16 waiting for the put-in of the camp we were to support.

- November 16 to Siple Station, 4.8 hours, some fuelling problems here, see Siple story

- November 16 to Byrd Surface Camp, 3.5 hours, overnight

- November 17 to Crary Ice Rise, the camp we would fly 322 hours from, prior to leaving for home on January 17

—

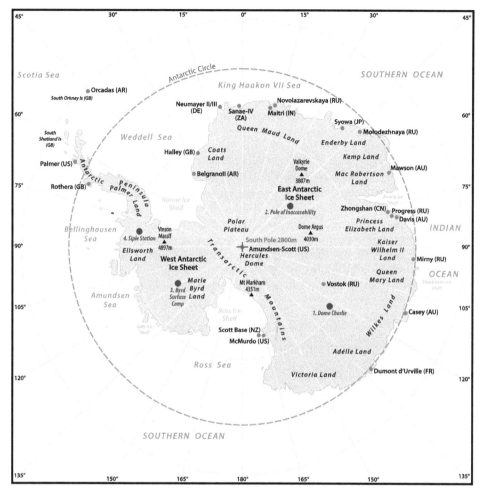

Figure 40. Shows some of the locations that I have talked about in this book. I added the following four locations:

1. Dome C or Charlie

2. the Pole of Inaccessibility

3. Byrd Surface Camp

4. Siple Station

Rothera

Rothera is the British Antarctica Survey Base located on the Antarctic Peninsula. We used it as a fuel stop and stayed overnight on the trips south when we were working for N.S.F. Its location, seven to eight hours south of Punta Arenas, Chile, meant we would hit a point of no return about four hours into our flight across the Drake Passage.

Weather conditions can change rapidly along the peninsula, but the forecast for our arrival still looked pretty good. Well, that was at our halfway point. By the time we were about an hour from Rothera, things had started to deteriorate rapidly. Luckily, there was open water around the Base and, with that as a reference, we were able to descend and circle over the open water in the sound. As this was our first trip into this location, we did not have much information on their ski strip, which was located on a glacier a few miles from camp. The radio operator advised us that there was a snowcat at the strip, and we would be able to land anywhere beyond it. As we circled inland from the open water, we spotted a black snowmobile sitting just beyond three rows of black flags and decided that must be it. We could not see any further up the glacier due to the worsening visibility and the whiteout conditions. Making one more circle while doing the landing checks, we touched down just beyond the snowmobile on what turned out to be quite a steep slope with one row of flags stretching out ahead of us. I called to say that we were down and got a reply saying they did not see us, had not even heard us, and where were we? Oops!

"We are along a single row of black flags that are just beyond a triple row of flags and a snowcat," I replied.

There was a long silence. "Don't move from there, we will be with you in about ten minutes," came the reply. Out of the fog came two snowmobiles, and they signalled us to follow them. After about three miles of steep undulating terrain, we arrived at the strip with the snowcat parked beside it. We had landed on what was marked as the traverse to the runway and were lucky to have not hurt the aircraft.

IFigure 41. This shows the traverse where we landed. X1 is where the broken snowmobile was parked, X2 is where we landed, X3 is the continuation of the traverse, over the horizon and on for another mile or so. The dark objects at the bottom of the glacier are the B.A.S. dog teams. It turned out that one of the snowmobiles had headed for the runway to meet us but had broken down and been abandoned just beyond the steepest part of the traverse. It was this that we took as a snowcat and based our landing on. I was the subject of much ribbing over the next week while we waited for conditions to improve for our departure. We always received a warm welcome there from the winter-over crew. The new faces and the boxes of fresh vegetables and fruit were more than welcome, and they provided an excuse for quite a party.

The Winter-Over Crew 1984

Figure 42. Rothera Base November 10, 1984. Clockwise from top left:

Pete Forman (cook), Dave Baker (Borek engineer), Andy Carter (air mechanic), Rob Day (tractor mechanic), Ron Irons (builder), Maurice O'Donnell (radioman), Pete Stark (weatherman), Ed Murton (B.A.S. chief pilot)

Harry Hanlan (Borek pilot), Alistair Cain (General Assistant), Chris O'Donoghue (pilot), Gerry Nicholson (logistics)

Bob Allan (Borek pilot), Rupert Summerson (General Assistant), Dick Hassler (B.A.S. pilot), Donny Stewart (General Assistant)

Siple Station

The radar picked up the twenty-three-mile-long antenna at a distance of forty miles and painted it as a narrow line across the screen. It slowly advanced towards us as we descended down to five hundred feet on the radar altimeter. The co-pilot Bob Allan and the engineer Dave Baker strained their eyes, trying to pick up some visual reference in the vast expanse of white while I stayed on instruments. This was the first time we had been to Antarctica, and we really had no idea what we were getting into. The meetings in Washington had made it sound quite simple. Fly about six hundred miles into the continent, locate the abandoned station of Siple, find and dig out the entrance, then crawl down a sixty-foot ladder to where a fuel bladder and a pump were located. Start the pump, then go back to surface and use the fuel hose that had been tied to an antenna mast to fuel the aircraft. Then, return the hose to the mast, crawl back down to the pump, shut everything down, and prepare for the next leg of the trip to Byrd Surface Camp where a crew and a bunk would be waiting for us.

The first indication of a problem was the lack of an antenna mast and a hose. Sometime during the winter, a storm had blown the mast over and buried the fuel hose. We had nothing to indicate which direction or distance from the entrance it would be, so to begin a probing exercise would seem pointless. We dug the entrance out and descended sixty darkening feet into the biggest deep-freeze you ever saw. Our flashlight beams got weaker as we located the bladder and pump. I'm not sure to this day that we would ever have started that cold-soaked pump. We had hoped there would be enough hose to reach to the surface and, in fact, there was. Problem was, the size and weight of it was beyond our ability to lift. Without fuel, we could go no further and decided the best bet would be to pitch our tents on surface and try to work out a game plan.

We were six hundred miles from anything, and to say I jumped at the call of, "Hola, ¿cómo está usted?" would be the understatement of the year. Turned out that the Chilean air force had dropped two men off a week earlier to look after the ground end of a fuel drop. They had dug into a small shack below the surface and were waiting for their Twin Otter to pick them up. They had been sleeping when we landed and only realized we were there when one climbed to surface for a pee. With our limited Spanish and their limited English, we managed to establish that the fuel drop had taken place in a seventy-mile-an-hour storm, and their fuel was scattered for miles, attached to shredded chutes and splintered pallets. Over a freeze-dried supper and a few bottles of Pisco, we explained our problem and sympathized with theirs. Many of the drums had been damaged in the drop and a second trip was going to be necessary for their requirements. To make a long story short, we agreed to swap six bottles of Pisco plus six bottles of wine for five barrels of fuel. The condition was that we had to use the damaged drums farthest from the camp. We arrived at Byrd Station the following day.

Figure 43. Borrowing fuel, Siple Station, 1984

Figure 44. Lowering supplies sixty feet to Siple Station, 1986

Field Camp

The following photos show our accommodation on the ice shelf in Antarctica.

Figure 45. Our first-year camp in Antarctica. The Jamesway was very noisy and cold.

Figure 46. The second year with the Jamesway about half buried was best of all.

Figure 47. Our third-year camp in Antarctica. This year, the Jamesway was very warm, very quiet, and no wind could be heard. It was a little awkward to get into, quite dark, but very comfortable.

In 1984, these units had no water, no shower, and the best you could do was melt a basin of snow on the Preway heater to have a warm wash in the morning. We would have six people in a 16 x 20 or 24-foot Jamesway, and most of us preferred the floor to the folding camp cots.

I think the biggest problem was having no washing facilities. You had to make whatever clothing you had last for over two months. Good thing the cold temperatures did not allow much for sweat. Plus, everyone was in the same predicament, so no one noticed. In the following years, we developed a snow melter that attached to a small pressure pump and a water heater that allowed a small shower to be installed in the rear entryway of the Jamesway. What also helped— as the other scientists heard of the work we were able to do with the Twin Otter, we were moved around to different camps. This often meant an overnight in McMurdo with a chance to do some laundry and get a shower.

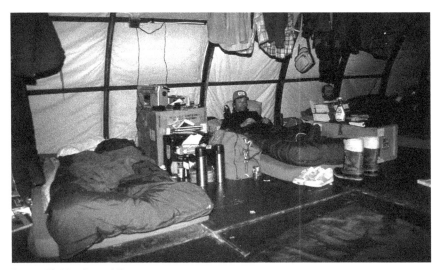

Figure 48. My allotted floor space

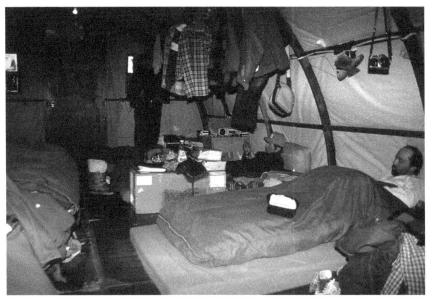

Figure 49. Dave and Bob enjoying the luxury.

Figure 50. Ground Storm

Figure 51. Morning after a storm when the Jamesway was on surface; once they were buried things were better.

Palmer Station

Figure 52. The Palmer winter-over crew. They had ordered the tuxedos months in advance for this wonderful shot, in penguin country.

I was ferrying a Twin Otter from Calgary to Antarctica in 1985 to work the summer season for the National Science Foundation. The weather forecast looked favourable for the seven-hour flight across the Drake Passage. But things change fast.

Well beyond the point of no return on our Punta Arenas to Rothera route, Rothera, the main British base in Antarctica, called to advise us that their weather was beginning to deteriorate, and the revised forecast did not look good for our planned arrival.

I had been talking to Palmer Station earlier in the flight, and they had jokingly asked if there was any chance we could stop at their location. I had told them we could not, as we had a bunch of aircraft control surface parts that the Brits were waiting for. The Brits' two Twin Otters had been turned upside down by a wind gust, and they were getting behind in their program. I now called Palmer back and asked about their strip condition and if they could supply us with some fuel. No one had used their strip in years, but they would send a snowcat up to drag it for us, and yes, they had some fuel.

What a warm welcome we received! Everyone but the radio operator and the cook were at the strip, and we were soon tied down and on our way to the base. Steak, Alaska king crab, champagne, and many bottles of red wine made this a most memorable stop. Next morning, the weather at Rothera had cleared, and after putting two barrels of rather dubious fuel into our tanks, we were on our way.

Mail and I Never Got Along That Well

I was flying air support in about 1974 for a seismic company north and west of Norman Wells in the Northwest Territories, and I had put a bundle of outbound mail in one of the zippered pockets of my flight suit.

When I got home that evening, there was a package of two new flight suits on the kitchen table. My old suit was quickly discarded while I tried on the new issue. A couple of months later, I was heading to the high Arctic for a two-month contract and was cleaning out the cupboard when I found my old flight suit on the floor with the packet of mail still in the pocket. Various visions of the problems that this had probably caused raced through my mind as I tried to solve this dilemma. Finally, deciding that late was better than never and not being the first person to lay the blame on Canada Post, I spread the letters out on the floor, left boot prints on each and every envelope, and took them to the post office. I'm not proud of this, but it seems like nothing compared to my next bad mail encounter.

It's 1986, and I'm flying for a couple of science groups that were working on the ice shelves in Antarctica. Very isolated camps with a Hercules flight coming in maybe once every couple of weeks. Now, at this time, there was no internet, phone, or any other means of communication other than snail mail. A letter written in camp sat in a bag for a week or two, then went to McMurdo where it would get onto the next plane to Christchurch. From there, a United States military plane would take it to the States where it would be put into the postal service. The replies followed the route in reverse, so the return time from camp could be between four and eight weeks.

I had taken the Otter into McMurdo for some reason, and on my return trip I was given a plastic grocery bag half full of mail for the camp. Eager for mail, there were quite a few people waiting as I taxied in to park—even though it was blowing a gale and in the -30°F range. As I passed the bag of mail out of the cockpit door, it fell to the ice, split open, and envelopes took off like leaves in a hurricane. Everyone watched in horror as everything, including the bag, disappeared into the blowing snow. Nothing was ever found, and it was a long time before I saw a smile in that camp.

Downstream Bravo

I've flown across the barren lands all
white with blowing snow,

I've flown across the Arctic ice as far as you can go.

I thought that I had seen all of the nothing you can see,

But man, you ain't seen nothing till
you've flown round *Downstream B.*

Figure 53. One of the ice streams
that run for miles and miles

Miles and Miles of Nothing

There are miles and miles of nothing here,

But miles and miles of more.

It's all the same, then back again,

My God, it's such a chore.

If it wasn't for the people here,

I don't think I'd return.

I'd stay at home and nurse the fire,

And watch the embers burn.

But here are friends to share a drink,

Perhaps a laugh or two.

And so, I keep on coming back,

My friend and so do you.

Figure 54. A Remote Antarctic Field Camp on the Ice Stream

Rothera Crash

November 1994. We had spent the day with the scientists who were studying emperor penguins in the vicinity of Terra Nova Bay, north of McMurdo. On the return flight, we stopped at the Italian base at Terra Nova for some fuel prior to heading to McMurdo. Weather conditions at McMurdo were bad, so, with only one day remaining to complete the work in the area, we decided to fly to the final location. The air crew would pitch a tent and get some required crew rest while the scientists finished off their program. Hopefully, the weather in McMurdo would clear in the eighteen to twenty-four-hour period we were planning.

Calling McMurdo on the H.F. radio, I explained our plans and revised our flight plan. Radio reception was deteriorating, but my message was received and confirmed. While we were refuelling, the base commander came down to the strip to tell me that one of our Twin Otters was arriving from Canada to do some work for them. It was at the British Base in Rothera, and they were expecting it to arrive within a few days.

We departed, flew a couple hours to the last penguin colony location, unloaded the science gear, pitched a tent, and crawled into our sleeping bags while the scientists headed out to finish their work.

About fifteen hours later, we were airborne, headed for McMurdo. When I called on the H.F. to pass my estimate, there was a long silence. Then, my friend Polly, sounding very strange, said, "Harry, is that you?"

"Yes, it's me."

Again, a long silence. Then, "Oh God, something's wrong here," then more silence. A few minutes passed, then the base manager was on the mike, telling me he would meet me at the airstrip.

The manager and the base chaplain met us at the strip and gave us the bad news. The airplane that was headed to Terra Nova Bay had crashed on takeoff from Rothera. All four on board had been killed. News of this accident had been passed to the base in Terra Nova who had then forwarded the information to McMurdo. With the bad radio reception, the broken English used by the Italians, and the timing of my departure from Terra Nova, McMurdo had understood from the message that it was my aircraft that had crashed on takeoff. It was an emotional roller coaster for the base as things slowly got straightened out.

Scared

I am often asked about scary moments during my flying career. I tend not to dwell on scary situations, but as some of my other stories unfold; to say I was never scared would be an out-and-out lie.

The scariest incident I was ever involved in did not include an airplane. It occurred on a day off in Antarctica when I booked to go out to some ice caves at the foot of a glacier outside of McMurdo.

The transport was a large snowcat, similar to the one pictured below. The rear section was accessible only through the rear door, and the unit we were in had a set of stairs, which swung up and were chained into position across the door at the rear. There was not an escape hatch in the roof, and there was no way to contact the driver or the two passengers in the front cab. Realizing that we were, in fact, locked into this thing, started to worry me as we headed out onto the ice. Unknown to any of us in the back, the driver, as I found out later, had never driven this route and was brand new to ice and snow. How this person was ever put into this position without some training remains a mystery to me.

I had been told the trip out would take about an hour. As that time span passed, we were still heading outbound, even though the glacier would be off to our right a mile or so. I have had a lot of experience on ocean ice, and the colour changes that we were encountering were worrying me no small amount. But, on and on we went. There was not a damn thing I could do but sit and watch this all unfold. It was obvious that the driver was confused and made a few turns looking for what, I will never know. Finally, she turned around and followed her tracks back to where she had missed the turnoff.

I flew over the route the next day. I am sure if had she continued another quarter mile, we would have been on ice unable to support the snowcat. I still get a scared feeling every time I tell this story. When you have no control over a situation that you know is going bad, it is scary.

Figure 55. A snowcat similar to the one used for the trips to the ice caves

The Blast

In Antarctica, when we were living in tents out on the ice streams, we used to melt a hole for the outhouse by drilling a four-inch hole about five feet deep. Then we would drop a couple rolls of toilet paper down the hole, pour in a couple of gallons of JP8 (diesel), and light the fuel. Within a few hours, there would be a hole roughly two feet in diameter and twenty or so feet deep over which we would place the outhouse. Usually, this worked very well. On one occasion, though, we melted down into a crevasse and ended up with an updraft that would flap your shirt-tails up your back and made it impossible to dispose of the toilet paper. We tried many schemes to alleviate the problem, but in the end, we abandoned it and drilled a new hole.

Figure 56. The coldest place on earth

One such hole was being melted one day when a young scientist from one of the southern states, he had a union flag with him, wandered over to the hole, decided that things weren't going fast enough, and proceeded to pour a two-gallon jug of gasoline down the hole. He had managed to get about half of it poured when it reached the bottom of the hole and exploded with considerable force. Enough to blow him and the jug of gas about twenty feet back from the hole. Luckily, he was uninjured, but he was the butt of many jokes after that.

We played one of the more memorable jokes on this same guy after he had spent the best part of his spare time over two weeks building an igloo, which he was planning on sleeping in the next night. To back up a bit, the seismic work was over, there was a surplus of powder to be disposed of, and we had been talking of having one big blast to get rid of it. Well, while our genius was away from camp, we buried the powder under his igloo and ran the wires under the snow to a spot some two-hundred-feet away, then we brought them to surface and back to the camp. That evening after supper, we drew straws to see who would activate the detonator and rigged the draw so that our friend won the right to push the plunger. Everyone was outside to witness the blast. With his eyes riveted to the end of the wires, he pushed the handle and the igloo disappeared into a column of snow and soot that reached hundreds of feet into the air. Too funny.

Figure 57. The Blast

Boondoggles

Operating in Antarctica, The National Science Foundation's fleet of ski-equipped C-130 Hercules aircraft, supplemented by a helicopter operation and some contracted Twin Otters, was the only air support that could effectively cover the continent. As such, they were often called on by other countries for rescue missions. They did not have total control on what occurs, but they still were expected to respond to emergency situations. Every incident caused a major disruption in the scheduled workload that had to be completed during the short summer season. Understandably, they tried to discourage any seemingly foolish or dangerous projects that were proposed on the continent.

In 1993, the Norwegians came up with what was thought of as a ridiculous boondoggle, consisting of a team of four people on four snowmobiles, travelling from the coast to the South Pole, where they would attempt to locate and retrieve Amundsen's tent, which had been left from the 1911 expedition. Against the advice of the United States, the project proceeded, and when they got south of 81°, they got into a huge crevasse field. Not long after that, a radio call came in, advising that the leader of the group had fallen into a crevasse with his snowmobile and the remaining members were trapped in a crevasse field. They were afraid to continue and afraid to turn around and go back.

A rescue mission was planned using a C-130 as a recon flight and a Twin Otter to ferry in a rescue team consisting of personnel from New Zealand and the United States and the required equipment. Circling the crevassed area, we were surprised that the Norwegians had gotten as far as they did before disaster struck. Instead of having their machines roped together and travelling in a line, they were spread out abreast of each other, and we could see many large holes that had opened up behind them. There was a single track leading southward from their tent that ended in a black hole. The C-130 reported that they had flown over the camp three or four times and there was no sign of life, a routine that we duplicated a few hours later with the same results. The decision was made that the rescue team would attempt to reach the tent—if it was possible for us to land somewhere in the area. Circling further and further from the tent, I finally chose what I thought was a safe area about three kilometres away.

Doing what we call a ski drag, touching down but not stopping, I circled back looking at my tracks. There was no sign of collapse and no holes, so I landed and taxied back down my tracks, only to see a large hole off to one side of my path. I stopped just beyond the hole, and the rescue team roped up inside the aircraft and stepped gingerly out onto the surface. They had not gone more than thirty feet in front of the plane, walking in the ski tracks, when the lead man went down into a crevasse. This was to be the first of about twenty times this happened before they reached the tent. Clark my engineer and I pitched a small tent in front of the aircraft and tried to get some sleep, though the situation we were in did not let that happen.

When the rescue team reached the tent, they found the remaining expedition members huddled inside. They seemed unaware that there had been aircraft circling, as no one even came out of the tent to meet the rescuers. Strange behaviour indeed. The survivors insisted on bringing all their equipment back to the plane, even though the rescue party advised them that it would be all we could do to get just them out of there.

—

One of the rescue party rappelled down to the body of the leader in the crevasse, confirmed him dead, and decided that it would be impossible to perform a recovery. The leader had gone out alone to scout a path, just another sign of inexperience and foolishness.

I talked on the radio to McMurdo and South Pole, advising them that the only way we could get out of this place would be to leave all excess gear behind, meaning our survival gear, rescue equipment, and all the survivor's equipment. McMurdo agreed. As it was just over five hundred miles to South Pole, we were also critical on fuel reserves, so the decision was made that a C-130 would remain at the Pole until we arrived— just in case we needed a fuel drop to make it back.

While the rescue team marked out what we hoped was a safe take-off area, we argued with the three survivors and pointed out that if our gear was staying behind, then their stuff sure as hell was not going on the aircraft.

Most of the camps on the continent were aware of our situation and were monitoring our progress; there was a collective sigh of relief when we finally called airborne. The Herc at the Pole waited 'till we landed, even though we had called to say we were assured of a safe arrival.

The survivors, who were now known as the Norwegian Crevasse Jumping Team, were flown to McMurdo by the C-130 and were waiting for a flight to Christchurch when we arrived. We saw them around town, but not one of them ever offered any thanks. Guess they were still pissed about their gear.

I still find it hard to believe that they sat in the tent with a Herc and an Otter flying low overhead, and no one came outside. If we had landed much further away, I think the rescue mission would have been aborted for that reason.

The following report taken from the Antarctic Journal, 1994, detailed the rescue.

After flying about 927 kilometres (500 nautical miles) the Twin Otter arrived at the accident site at about 7:40 a.m. on 29 December (1:40 p.m. EST, 28 December) and landed about 3.2 kilometres from the site. Flying above the landing site, the SAR team could see numerous collapsed snow bridges and the distinct tracks of four snowmobiles crossing the crevasse field. The Norwegian camp was in sight, but no signs of life were evident. About 90 meters from the camp, the team saw a crevasse with ropes going down into it.

Despite the large number of crevasses that were apparent from the air, the pilots of the Twin Otter and the SAR team were not fully aware of the severity of the crevassing until they had landed. Although the pilots successfully and safely landed, they soon discovered that crevasses surrounded them. A quick evaluation of the situation brought an equally quick decision-the Twin Otter pilots would only take off from the spot; they would never land there again. All hope for shuttling the remaining SAR team members from the South Pole and getting additional equipment and assistance was gone.

At 8:30 a.m. local time, the rescue team, dragging a stretcher filled with first aid supplies and minimal crevasse rescue gear, began its approach on foot to the accident site. Within 30 meters of the Twin Otter, SAR coordinator Steve Dunbar fell into a 1-meter-wide crevasse-an event that foreshadowed the difficulties they were yet to encounter. The 3-kilometer traverse took them 4 hours during which members of the rescue team fell in crevasses more than 20 times. The closer they came to the camp, the bigger and more chaotic were the

—

crevasses. They also found that, despite the generally flat terrain of the area, they could not navigate by line-of-sight. Two 3- meter-high rises between the camp and the airplane forced them to use GPS navigation (navigation aided by Global Positioning Satellite).

Arrival at the camp presented them with an additional sur-prise-a second man had been injured earlier when he rode his snowmobile into a crevasse and had fallen more than 70 meters. While the Navy corpsman examined this man, who appeared to have a concussion and several cracked ribs, the rest of the rescue team made radio contact with South Pole Station and prepared for the final 90-meter traverse during which they encountered four more large crevasses.

The victim had fallen through a 1.2 meter-wide hole in a snow bridge. A quick visual evaluation of-the site revealed that a snowmobile had crossed and broken the bridge earlier about 9 meters to the left of the fall site. With his rope anchored to one of the Norwegian snowmobiles, SAR team leader Dunbar began his descent into the crevasse. He was able to rappel about 38 meters down the side of the crevasse. Here, the cre-vasse had narrowed to a width of only 20 centimetres; the temperature was nearly -35°C. About 1.5 meters below him, Dunbar could see the victim's arm protruding through snow that had fallen down the crevasse and buried him. Near the body, a sleeping bag, lowered to the victim by his compan-ions, lay untouched. There was no discernible sign of life. Because the narrowing crevasse prevented him from reaching the fallen man, Dunbar determined that they would not be able even to extricate the body.

Returning to the Norwegian camp, the SAR team informed South Pole Station that the Norwegian was dead and that they would not be able to retrieve the body. Their next task

—

was to prepare the surviving Norwegians for the traverse and explain the principles of roped travel to them. Because of the difficulties that they experienced during their trip to the camp and because of the airplane's weight restrictions, they took with them only the most essential gear. After a 3.5-hour traverse, they arrived at the landing site at which point the SAR team abandoned all gear except their survival equipment and a few pieces of SAR gear so that the Twin Otter could take off more easily. At 1:00 a.m. on 30 December, the SAR team, the Norwegian survivors, and the two Twin Otter pilots landed at Amundsen-Scott South Pole Station, the rescue mission completed. (*Antarctic Journal of the United States* Volume 29, no. 2, [June 1994] 11-12.)

For more information on this mission, perform a Google search on *Norwegian Antarctic Accident*.

The Pole of Inaccessibility

We had flown out to pick up some scientific equipment that had been circling the continent, suspended under a balloon which had landed at the hardest place to reach in Antarctica. The Hercs could not operate in the area. The elevation was just over twelve thousand feet and the terrain was very rough, so we were sent to do the recovery. Being way beyond our range of operation, it required an airdrop of fuel for us to get home. We landed and loaded the piece of freight, about eight hundred pounds, I think. I know we skidded it up a ramp with a come-along attached to an anchor that we had buried in the snow on the opposite side of the aircraft. It was tiring work at that altitude, but the worst was yet to come.

When the Herc arrived overhead to drop our fuel, we asked him to drop it ahead of the aircraft about half a mile. They had trouble opening the rear door of the Herc, and, for a while, it looked like they might have to abort the mission, which would have left us stranded. However, they finally got the door open and dropped our fuel about a mile off to the right of the aircraft on a very rough area. We had no choice but to taxi over to it. We had been asked to return the parachute and the pallet that the drums were on.

Well, at that altitude, all the chute did was keep the load upright, and it buried the drums about ten feet in the hard-packed snow. Digging down to the drums through the chute lines and nylon was the hardest work I have ever done. Two shovelfuls of snow, then stop and gasp for breath. When we finally got down to the drums, we just put an axe through the top or side of the drum, whatever we could see, and pumped the fuel out from the bottom of the of the pit. Good thing we had enough hose to reach. The chute and pallet were left behind.

It was always a bit of a risk getting an airdrop of fuel for a return flight because we had to go out first, find a suitable landing area, then call the Herc to come. If they had any mechanical problems or the weather closed in, we were stuck and damn cold.

See map page 139

DC-4 Ferry Flight to Chile

In October of 1990, we loaded up the DC-4 with spares, two engineers, two pilots, a co-pilot, my wife, who would be our radio operator once we got to Punta Arenas, Chile, and the wife of one of the engineers with her two caged cats. She was catching a ride with us as far as Toronto, where we were scheduled to pick up a spare engine. The cats were locked in the bathroom, and we endured their howls above the rumble of the engines for the full flight.

The only person we could find with any DC-4 experience was an old captain out of Vancouver who had lots of time on type, but was totally out of touch with I.F.R. Much to our dismay, he showed up just before our departure with his thirty-year-old challenged son.

Approaching Toronto, I asked Colin to fly while I looked over approach procedures. The fact that he had flown beyond our clearance point and was headed away from the approach beacon caused some problems when I took over control again.

Finally getting established on the I.L.S., we discovered that the weather was causing some major problems. It was the worst storm of the year for Toronto, and the aircraft ahead of us cancelled his approach and headed for his alternate. We continued the approach, and Colin called that *he had the lights*. I called for the gear down and some flaps before I looked out, to realize that he was looking at a freeway, not the airport. It took full power to continue the approach. As we were taxiing in, the storm hit in full fury, and one of our engines just up and quit. Sure glad it held on until we landed. One of our engineers quit right after the landing and took the next available flight back to Calgary. We now had to wait in Toronto for three days while we arranged an engine change and the purchase an additional engine. The only happy part of this was that we finally were rid of those howling cats.

The old captain with all the experience had been complaining of the poor performance of the aircraft. We did a recalculation of the load and all was within limits.

We finally got out of Toronto and landed at Miami, where they parked us next to the Concord. What a contrast—the rain and lights glistening off the beautiful white supersonic plane sure looked good compared to the old, oil-dripping DC-4. I went to the airport early the next morning to get a picture, but the Concord had left.

The next day found us in Guayaquil, Ecuador, and the takeoff in the hot weather was a pretty scary event. We had a close inspection of the roofs of the city as we slowly gained altitude.

The aircraft had been fitted with three extra fuel tanks to allow for the twenty-plus-hour return trip to the ice from Punta Arenas, and we had asked the engineer if, in fact, they were empty, which he confirmed three separate times. Turns out, they were right full and were the cause of the sluggish performance.

We had originally been cleared to Lima, Peru, on an airway that required us to be at nineteen thousand feet, which was impossible for the DC-4, as we had no oxygen on board. I thought we had cleared that up, and we would proceed at a low level along the coastline, one mile offshore, as we had done in the past with the Twin Otter.

Landing in Lima, we were met by an official who advised us that we *had entered his country illegally* and would not be able to fuel or proceed, and we must come to his office immediately. Margo was following me across the ramp with a paper bag full of cash when I heard a familiar voice calling my name. Jose McPherson, a guy I had met the year before, came running up to greet us. As I explained my concerns to him, he assured me that he could fix it all, and, in fact, he had fuel trucks headed for the aircraft within minutes.

The official was, in fact, pretty low on the totem pole, and we ended up paying him a small percentage of what he had been demanding. Walking back to the DC-4, I thanked Jose and slipped him a couple hundred dollars. I don't know what would have happened without his help. We were soon on our way and glad to say good-bye to Peru.

We blew a tire on landing at Antofagasta, Chile, and stopped in the centre of the only runway, closing the airport down completely. It took two long hours with the help of the Chilean military to get the plane jacked up and the tire replaced. The sun was coming up by the time we got to the hotel.

On to Santiago where we met up with the Chilean general who was working for Adventure Network to make their operation possible. Political bullshit at its finest.

A late start the next day put us south of Puerto Montt, crossing the Andes in the dark with some freezing rain, and no contact with Punta Arenas. We finally had to turn back and land at Puerto Montt, where we stayed for the remainder of the night.

Finally arriving in Punta Arenas late the next afternoon, we spent a week off-loading, locating some hanger space for our spare engine and other parts, renting a house big enough to house the crew, and renting a couple of cars.

We lived there for four months and did seventeen crossings of the Drake Passage to the camp at 80° S 80° W, where we landed on the tongue of a glacier that was blown clear of snow and polished by the wind.

Engine Fire

The DC-4 I was flying out of Punta Arenas, Chile, to the Antarctic continent was not quite big enough for the job we were trying to do. But, that's the case no matter how big a plane you have. With four 1,450 horsepower Pratt and Whitney engines and a maximum payload of thirty thousand pounds, it was a nice airplane but not quite what we needed. By the time we loaded sufficient fuel for the return flight, the cargo load was not all that much. Consequently, our departures from Punta were always on the heavy side of maximum.

The engineers had hung a new engine on the aircraft after we returned from the last flight with only three engines running. The ground runs and trial flight had gone well, and we were loaded and ready for the next trip. Taxiing out and lining up for takeoff, everything looked good. We were paying a lot of attention to the new engine during the takeoff run and, as we lifted off, one of the other engines failed and caught fire. Full emergency power on the three remaining engines gave us just enough power to clear the tops of the scrub pines at the end of the runway.

It must have been quite a show for the airport Kid's Day celebration. Here is a big orange and white airplane taking off, then circling back dumping a vapour cloud of excess fuel, and spewing flames from one engine. It was not much fun for the crew inside the aircraft or the ground crew members who were watching in horror. We had to do two circuits out over the bay to dump enough fuel to get below the maximum landing weight, and it seemed to take forever. Finally, we were able to land and the fire crew, who had been busy foaming the runway, chased us to a stop and extinguished the flames. Future takeoffs were on the light side of maximum.

Margo our radio operator always watched our departure and then went to the airport restaurant for a coffee before heading back to town to do the flight following. This day, when she walked into the restaurant, they met her at the door with a double Scotch. "Here, Miss Margot, today you need this".

Heavy Icing

I was based in Punta Arenas in southern Chile, flying supplies and people to a camp six hundred miles from the South Pole in Antarctica. The camp was a tourist operation that catered to mountaineers who were attempting to add Mount Vinson Massif to their Seven Summit mountain-climbing records. The crew consisted of two pilots, two engineers, and a base radio operator.

The round trip from Punta Arenas, Chile, to the base in Antarctica at 80 degrees south took about twenty-four hours, including one hour on the ice—unloading, fuelling, and reloading the DC-4. With the cold temperatures, we were reluctant to remain on the ice any longer. Today had been a good trip, and we were about two hours out of Punta with all four engines still turning. About two hundred miles south of the southern tip of South America and at ten thousand feet, we began running into an icing layer and climbed above it, only to find ourselves running into it again after another fifty miles. Again, we climbed above it, knowing that the bases of the clouds were below the minimum altitude we needed. Another fifty miles and we were forced again to climb, but this time we could not stay above it. As we entered the cloud, the aircraft started to collect ice fairly rapidly.

Ice is never welcome, but with the light load and four engines turning I felt confident that we could get over the highest peaks and melt off during the descent into Punta. The company's decision to remove the de-icing equipment from the aircraft to facilitate some extra payload had seemed like a good idea at the time.

Not so just now, as the accumulation of ice suddenly increased. We were now at full climb power and unable to maintain altitude. Punta's radar controller called to tell us that we must maintain ten thousand feet for the next sixty miles. "Well that's not too good," I replied, "we are at 9,800 and descending."

"You must maintain for terrain clearance, and I will lose contact with you shortly. Turn to heading 030° now, and if you lose contact, fly that heading for ten minutes, then turn to 350° for..." (static).

"Great, just great." We flew the 030° heading as suggested, then turned to 350°. You could feel the unseen peaks going by as we sank through 7,500 feet.

Finally, a hole appeared with water below it, and we managed a circling descent into some warmer air where we continued up and down the fiord until the ice melted off. Now, unsure of our exact position, we had to climb back up into the icing to finish the trip. At nine thousand feet, Radar Control again picked us up and advised that in twenty miles we would be able to descend to 7,500 feet, and lower shortly after that.

The parking ramp and Margo, with a case of cold beer, looked especially good that morning. Our normal procedure was to release Margo our radio operator about an hour and a half prior to our e.t.a. (estimated time of arrival), so she could meet us. Luckily, she had missed all the conversations during our ordeal.

There is a bit more to this story. The Punta airport staff had invited us to their monthly get-together and bingo game that night. During a few drinks and while the numbers were being called out twice, once in English for us, a man came up and introduced himself as Moncho. "Captain Hanlan, I am Moncho. I was working the radar this morning. I was very happy to see you reappear on my screen." After I proposed a toast to this man who had saved our lives, Moncho and I shared a bottle of Scotch, one of many shared over the years.

—

Figure 58. CF-IQM DC-4 on the ice in Antarctica 1988-89

Figure 59. CF-IQM DC-4 on the ice in Antarctica 1988-89

My Friend Ernie

I drove over to Vernon in October 2013 to see my old friends Ernie and Lee Christensen from Norman Wells. Ernie is in an assisted living facility and has a memory problem. As Lee and I sat with him and talked of some of the times we had had together, Ernie was actually able to join us from time to time. Lee told of a trip she had made with me some thirty years before that I had forgotten about.

The Single Otter on floats is a pretty slow old bird, and I used to read pocket books, tearing the page off after I finished it, so I could resume without thumbing through the book to find my place. Well, I guess I was reading away as we flew towards Colville Lake when one of the three fuel tanks ran dry. The sudden silence was terrifying to Lee, who was sitting in the right seat. She said what really made her mad was that I didn't even look up from my book, but just reached over and turned the fuel selector handle, then continued reading as if nothing had happened. I always ran the tank I was using dry, so I didn't have to come back to it if fuel became a problem.

I told a story that Ernie related to, about a time we had gone hunting caribou with a couple rifles that we had not sighted in. We fired about four shots each with no hits, and finally the caribou got bored and wandered away. Lee said that was the maddest she had ever seen Ernie, even madder than the morning he discovered I had cut off half of his handlebar moustache in the bar the night before. We had some wonderful times together over the years, and I sure teared up when I left him last week.

Figure 60. Ernie and I Oct, 2013.

Tom's Story

You have all read about Tom in my previous stories, and I am including a story written by Tom about one of our many exploits.

Figure 61. The first annual Lake Hazen Golf and Tundra Tournament. if you squint really hard, I'm squatting, about second or third from the left and Harry is the tall guy with the blue Pacific Western Airlines hat. He's second from the right in the back row

A long time ago, in a place far, far away, a group of friends got together to play a round of golf. In the mix were biologists, corporate owners, pilots, airline agents, air traffic controllers, kids, cat skinners, a representative from the Houston Armadillo Breeders and Growers Society, a member of the RCMP, a school teacher, and even a gentleman from Madras, India.

Nothing too unusual, I suppose. But this round of golf was called the *First Annual Lake Hazen Golf and Tundra Tournament*, and the location was exactly 410 nautical miles from the geographic North Pole. The gathering was hosted by Harry Hanlan and myself. Harry and I did a lot of travelling together over the years, and we had garnered a bit of a reputation, some of it true.

The location was a camp owned by Kenn Borek Air, the outfit that employed both Harry and myself. A loose collection of three tent structures around a plywood core that had been built in the 1950s and resurrected, mostly by Hanlan and Frook, in the late 1960s as a jumping-off or staging post for overnight guests who were going to the North Pole in the spring of each year. It wasn't the Hilton. Hell, it was probably not even on par with the Gull Motel in Gull Lake, Saskatchewan. But given the location and the fact that it had oil heat and a fairly serviceable Esso oil-bucket bathroom, Lake Hazen Camp was pretty much *uptown*.

Harry and I had finished the spring tours to the Pole. I don't remember how many we'd done that year, and it doesn't matter. But, at the conclusion of the tours, the two of us were sitting around the hangar in Resolute Bay, reflecting on the success of the spring tours and wondering what we could do to lessen the enormous workload for future years. The tours to the Pole weren't easy. They were awfully hard work that involved hauling everything that was needed to support the tourists, the crews, and the aircraft, plus keeping in mind the ever-possible need for evacuation. You can't likely grasp just how hard this was, moving over two hundred drums of fuel, food, bedding, radios, batteries, and liquor, while also making absolutely certain that there was sufficient toilet paper for the length of the tour plus a reserve. For everything that was hauled north to Lake Hazen, a similar amount of waste and garbage had to be hauled south at the conclusion—so, a huge chore.

So, the germ of an idea began to take shape. It may have been after the first bottle of Dewar's or maybe the second, but we thought that it would be nice if we could somehow show our appreciation to those folks in the north who had helped us and to invite some of our favourite tourists to return to the Arctic (at their own expense). We'd all go to Lake Hazen for a golf tournament. What could possibly be better? Neither of us could see anything wrong with the idea, at least at that moment. What we'd obviously missed was the fact that we'd somehow have to use a Twin Otter that usually went for $3.60 per mile plus fuel at ninety gallons an hour, the groceries, the liquor, and all the peripherals. And somehow, we'd have to make sure that none of the escapade made it to paper for future reference. We considered calling it *training time*, but that would require an entry in the log book, and we didn't want that; so, I decided that we'd call it *prepaid expenses* towards the next year's tours. The strange thing was that the Dawson Creek accounting office actually bought it.

The invitations were extended and sometime in July of, maybe 1977, friends from the south began arriving in Resolute Bay to make ready for the tournament. Harry ran a quick load to Lake Hazen, a one-way trip of almost eight hundred miles, hauling fuel and groceries, so that we'd have sufficient room on the aircraft for the golfers and their gear. Late one Friday night (remember, the sun doesn't set in the summer), we loaded the Twin Otter with a good bunch of friends and made our way to Lake Hazen by way of the Inuit community of Grise Fiord on Ellesmere Island. It was in Grise Fiord that a lot of us put our hands on the necessary items for golf at the Grise Fiord Eskimo Co-op, the only store in town, in fact, the only store on Ellesmere Island. For obvious reasons, golf clubs and golf balls weren't readily available in Grise Fiord, so we made do with what was available, things like hockey sticks, rubber tennis balls, extra large children's plastic baseball bats, anything really that would hit a ball. And, away we went, Lake Hazen just a mere four hundred miles distant.

The Lake Hazen airport was a little piece of hilltop, about thirty-five feet wide and, perhaps, four hundred feet long. It was also muddy. It mattered not. We arrived safely, unloaded, and retired to the nineteenth hole to make ready for the tournament. A wonderful nine-hole course was laid out towards the West, along the shore of the lake between the Ruggles River and the camp . If you played what we thought might be a par game, that par would be about 260, maybe more. Rubber balls whacked with hockey sticks and bouncing off rocks that have been permanently frozen for millions of years tend to go wherever they want. As I remember, we all played a round. I have no idea who may have been the winner, but likely it would be the same person who had the fewest visits to the nineteenth hole.

We fished for Arctic char in the lake and in the Ruggles River, which, incidentally, never freezes, despite being just a short hop from the Pole. The pitch of the land, as it falls into the Greenland Straits, is such that the water doesn't have a chance to slow down enough to freeze. The river empties at Fort Conger, a pit stop for early polar explorers.

The trip back to Resolute Bay was far more subdued than had been the northbound leg of the journey. Most folks were pretty weary and were looking forward to things like showers and toilets that weren't lined with black garbage bags.

The photo that's attached came to me two days ago from Harry Hanlan. That's what prompted me to tell you about the tournament. But looking at the picture, I'm amazed at just how few of the golfers are left. Damned few. I can't understand just how we, meaning Harry and me, managed to get away with a lot of these pranks—the pot was kept pretty well stirred, and there weren't many days that we didn't have something cooked up for entertainment. I'm certainly glad to still be in touch with my old chums who were part of that group. We check on each others well-being and have the occasional laugh.

Acknowledgments

I would like to thank Margo

for her support and encouragement.

Without her this book would never have happened.

I would also like to thank

Liesl and Greg Hanlan for all their help.